PAGANISM AND CHRISTIANITY
IN EGYPT

T0382528

ISIS AND HORUS

From a Graeco-Roman ivory in the British Museum
No. 26255 (see p. 140 f.)

PAGANISM AND
CHRISTIANITY IN EGYPT

by

PHILIP DAVID SCOTT-MONCRIEFF
M.A. CANTAB.

Cambridge :
at the University Press
1913

CAMBRIDGE UNIVERSITY PRESS
Cambridge, New York, Melbourne, Madrid, Cape Town,
Singapore, São Paulo, Delhi, Mexico City

Cambridge University Press
The Edinburgh Building, Cambridge CB2 8RU, UK

Published in the United States of America by Cambridge University Press, New York

www.cambridge.org
Information on this title: www.cambridge.org/9781107668904

First published 1913
First paperback edition 2013

A catalogue record for this publication is available from the British Library

ISBN 978-1-107-66890-4 Paperback

PREFACE

THE little work which is now given to the public
was produced by a scholar whose sudden death in
February 1911, before he had completed his twenty-
ninth year, came as a painful surprise to his many
friends. After a training in Semitic languages at
Cambridge, he entered the British Museum in Decem-
ber 1903, becoming an assistant in the department of
Egyptian and Assyrian antiquities. From that time
his attention was mainly given to Egyptian research
(including a visit to Egypt), but he also found time to
edit an important Syriac text—the letters of Îshô'-
yahbh—which issued from the press in 1904. His
friends and colleagues, Mr Leonard W. King and Mr
H. R. Hall, have acted as editors of the present volume
and have supplied the following summary of his other
work during his service in the Museum. In October
and November of 1905 he was engaged, in conjunction
with Mr J. W. Crowfoot, in clearing out the XVIIIth
dynasty temple at Wady Ḥalfa, of which he published
a description, with plan and photographs, in the *Proc.
Soc. Bibl. Arch.*, Jan. 9, 1907, pp. 39 ff. This work was
undertaken on behalf of the Sudan Government on the

recommendation of Dr E. A. Wallis Budge. In 1909 he published a discussion of Plutarch's treatise *De Iside et Osiride* in the *Journal of Hellenic Studies*, XXIX. pp. 79 ff. He has also contributed reviews of Oriental books to *The Church Quarterly Review, The Burlington Magazine, The Classical Review, The Journal of Hellenic Studies*, and *The Morning Post*. He was a contributor to the *Encyclopaedia of Religion and Ethics*, his most considerable article being that on the *Coptic Church*. At the time of his death he had just completed Part I. of an official publication of the British Museum, entitled *Hieroglyphic Texts from Egyptian Stelae &c. in the British Museum.*

The present work was very nearly completed at the time of the author's death, but had not received his final corrections. It is known that he intended to write an additional chapter summarising his conclusions, but no trace of this has been found among his papers. Hence two sentences have been added within brackets on p. 219 in order to round off the chapter. A few additions have also been made in the rest of the volume and placed within brackets, and any references which were wanting have been filled in. The editors have been assisted in the reading of the proofs by two other of Scott-Moncrieff's friends and colleagues, Messrs G. F. Hill and O. M. Dalton, and by myself.

Mr King has also been kind enough to supply the following notes on the archaeological interest of the book.

" Apart from its value as a handbook, the originality of the work, in our opinion, consists chiefly in two features. In the first place Scott-Moncrieff approached his subject from the Egyptian point of view. He had a first-hand knowledge of the ancient Egyptian religion and was thus peculiarly fitted to detect the changes from native belief, which were introduced in the Graeco-Roman cults of Egyptian divinities, and had so strong an influence on early Christian thought in Egypt. In the second place, as an archaeologist, he was able to form his own estimate of the bearing of the archaeological upon the purely literary evidence, and in several cases to use his data in a novel way. As an instance we may cite his critical discussion of Monsieur Gayet's excavations of Christian graves at Antinoë during the years 1896—1900, and his correction of the late date assigned to them by their discoverer. Scott-Moncrieff was certainly right in using them as evidence of the character of Egyptian Christianity during a period at least a century earlier. Again, Forrer's publication of Christian objects from Akhmim is of greater scientific value, but the fact that they were obtained by native diggers necessarily leaves many problems of dating, etc. open to discussion. Scott-Moncrieff has pointed out the bearings of the principal Akhmim finds upon his subject, and his handling of the evidence will do much to clear up uncertainties and to suggest points on which fresh evidence will be welcome.

"In his descriptions and summaries of the early Gnostic literature he has been able to make interesting suggestions with regard to the origin of some of the magical words of power. And his summary of the earlier literary and documentary evidence, bearing on the beginnings of Christianity in Egypt, should prove a useful introduction to the subject and a guide to the literature."

The book bears everywhere the impress of its author's keen, fresh mind and attractive personality. It should prove useful and stimulating to many students of early Christian literature, bringing them into touch with factors in the early development of Christian ideas and institutions which are not easily discerned by those whose reading is confined to Greek and Latin authors. Scott-Moncrieff was one who in a short time accomplished much: and while we mourn that his career was so suddenly interrupted, we cannot be too thankful for what he has left us.

N. M^cLEAN.

CHRIST'S COLLEGE,
     CAMBRIDGE.
          March 1913.

CONTENTS

CHAPTER I

THE EGYPTIAN RELIGION AT THE CLOSE
OF THE PTOLEMAIC ERA

THE history of Christianity during the two centuries following the apostolic era is everywhere obscure, and nowhere more so than in Egypt, for, although it is true that we have in the early patristic literature many glimpses of the growth of the new faith and its rapid increase throughout the provinces of the Roman empire, we know hardly anything about the conversion of the peasantry and lower strata of society outside the great Hellenistic centres. Presbyters, bishops, martyrs, and apologists, all imbued with the spirit of hellenism and educated under Hellenic influence, are the main personalities from whom we derive our conception of the progress of Christianity. Yet it should not be forgotten that in Asia Minor and Egypt, hellenism was only a veneer covering lower strata which were essentially oriental and had inherited civilizations and religions far more ancient than anything Greek. In Asia Minor, especially in the great towns near the Mediterranean, Greek influence had permeated deeply the life of all classes, and a large number of the religious cults had become hellenized, but this was not the case in Egypt, who at the time of her incorporation into the Roman empire maintained her national characteristics and above all her ancient religion hardly touched by Hellenic influence. Even Alexandria, which was perhaps the most perfect type of the later Greek city and had been for three hundred years the court of the Ptolemies and the centre of Hellenic philosophy and learning, was deeply imbued with Egyptian religious ideas, paying great veneration to such deities as Serapis, Isis and Osiris. And the further the traveller who had taken ship in Alexandria sailed up the Nile, the less noticeable the influence of the Greeks became. Soon he would come to towns and villages where indeed the administrative machinery set up by the Ptolemies was carried on in Greek, but where Greek ideas and Greek methods were still foreign. On either side of the river he would find towns dominated by vast temples controlled by powerful priestly gilds, and a people given over to an elaborate religion which seemed to the Greek merely a superstitious veneration for certain animals. Many of the temples and the cults connected with them were of very great antiquity and the priests would tell the travelling stranger legends of the ancient greatness of Egypt. For here in the valley of the Nile was a people, heir of the oldest civilization in the world, worshipping its ancient gods and continuing its immemorial customs little influenced by Greek or Roman activity, and having only two things in common with the other provinces of the empire: taxes were paid and the emperors were officially worshipped. Such was Egypt in the time of Augustus Caesar. Nevertheless, in 250, the edict of Decius against Christians revealed the fact that Christianity had spread far and wide, not only among the inhabitants of Alexandria but everywhere else in Egypt, especially among the native population whose faith in its own gods had never hitherto been shaken. How the new religion increased and the old beliefs fell into decay, and the effect of the new faith on a stubborn and conservative people, forms one of the most interesting chapters in the history of religion.

When, as the result of the battle of Actium and the defeat of Cleopatra, Egypt passed into the possession of Octavianus Caesar, the country had been for three centuries under Hellenic rule. The city founded by Alexander the Great and made magnificent by the first Ptolemies had become the first Hellenistic city of the world, for Alexandria with its Museum and Library was the centre of Greek learning and scarcely second to Athens herself. Its position as the harbour of export for the corn trade of Egypt and the products of Africa made it a city of enormous commercial activity, and its streets were thronged with merchants of every nationality, Greeks, Jews, Egyptians, and all the peoples of Syria and Asia Minor. Nevertheless its geographical position prevented any rapid hellenization of Egypt itself. Lying at the extreme northern point of a country which may best be described as a long riband of cultivated land formed by the Nile in the midst of surrounding deserts, it occupied the worst possible position for enlarging its sphere of influence. It is, therefore, not a matter of surprise that at the end of the Ptolemaic era the native Egyptians still maintained their national characteristics to a large extent intact, in

spite of a Greek administration and a large influx of
foreigners. This was particularly the case with their
most pronounced national trait, their devotion to their
religion. It has often been the custom of Egyptologists
to look on the Ptolemaic period as one of decline, as a
"basse époque," but it becomes more and more evident
that in some ways it was a period of great national
revival, especially in religious matters. The Ptolemies
not only gave the country firm and settled government,
but, knowing well the great power wielded by the priests,
proclaimed themselves the benefactors of the national
religion. In consequence, not only were the revenues
of the old religious centres such as Thebes, Memphis
and Bubastis restored to something of their former
wealth, but vast building projects were undertaken and
carried out during the reigns of successive monarchs, as
at Dendera, Edfu, Philae and elsewhere ; so that after
the lean and stormy years of Persian domination the
great gilds of priests found themselves once more in
a position of wealth and security. In return for this
patronage and support the priests showed the utmost
loyalty to the Greek kings, as we know by such
documents as the Decree of Canopus and the proclamation on the Rosetta Stone. Divine honours were
paid to them and everywhere they were represented
on the temple walls wearing the prescribed garments
of the old kings when worshipping the gods, bearing
the royal protocols of their native predecessors, and
adoring and making offerings to the ancient deities of
the land of Egypt. Where the priests led the people
followed, and though revolts of the natives broke out
during the reigns of Ptolemy IV and Ptolemy V, the

Egyptians seem on the whole to have been well content under Greek rule so long as they were free from invasion and able to worship their gods after the manner of their forefathers.

Being thus in a position of security and wealth, the great priestly colleges turned their attention to the complicated doctrines and rituals of their ancient religion. The erection of new temples throughout the country stimulated not only their skill as architects and craftsmen, but also their researches into the religious legends and lore of the past. They were once more able to conduct the worship of the gods with fitting pomp and ceremony, and this led them to make investigations into the old religious literature in search of authority for their doctrines and usages. The consequence was that the elaborate rites of the old religion were carried on during this period in what was deemed by the priests the manner prescribed from time immemorial by generations of their forefathers. In reality the religious ceremonies described by the Ptolemaic inscriptions must have been even more elaborate than the great sacred processions and ceremonies of the XVIIIth and XIXth dynasties, as the Ptolemaic priests in their antiquarian zeal seem to have left no stone unturned in their search for ritualistic minutiae and correctness. But it was nevertheless significant that all the ceremonial connected with the various cults was described in detail on the temple walls for the first time. Hitherto this had not been necessary. Now the people of Egypt had forgotten, or were beginning to forget, the meaning of these ceremonies, and the priests themselves had to be informed by the more learned of their order, with whom knowledge alone lay. It is thus that we have the first glimpse even early in Ptolemaic times of the rift which gradually grew greater between the priestly schools of the great religious centres and the common people; as time went on, the tendency became more and more marked for the priests to become learned societies with whom alone rested the knowledge of the doctrines of the old religion, while the population at large, although indeed keeping their old beliefs, became worshippers of a few favourite gods and open to the influence of hellenism.

This cleavage had become clearly marked at the beginning of the Roman epoch. Although it seems evident that in the great temples the priests still carried on the worship of the gods with all the due rites and ceremonies prescribed by past ages, and although the people flocked to watch the great religious processions and took part in them on great occasions such as the visit of one deity to another, it is nevertheless probable that the general population understood little of the inner meaning of all these rites. Nor were the explanations and details inscribed in hieroglyphics on the walls of much assistance, for the hieroglyphic script was no longer understood by the ordinary scribes and people who could read, the demotic script having long since taken its place for every day purposes. Indeed, the hieroglyphs of the Ptolemaic period had plainly ceased to be the vehicle of ordinary speech, for the priests took delight in making them as fantastic as possible, so that it would have puzzled a good scribe of the middle or new empire to make head or tail of them.

So it came about that, in spite of the religious activity that had taken place throughout Egypt under the Ptolemies, the religion of the people generally began to shew those signs of decay which ultimately led to the rapid degeneration of the second and third centuries and paved the way for the speedy growth of Christianity. The study of this popular religion and of its waning hold over the people of Egypt is of considerable importance when discussing the problems connected with the early days of Christianity, and, as archaeologists in recent years have done a great deal to throw light on the subject, it will be as well to examine it in some detail.

In Roman times, as formerly, the most salient feature of the religion of the Egyptians seems to have been the worship of the gods of the dead and the belief that it was possible for the dead to live again an eternal existence in the world of spirits. They based their belief in this on the legends which centred round their principal god of the dead, Osiris, and fortunately we have an account of the legend as it was generally accepted in Roman times in Plutarch's work *de Iside et Osiride.* Plutarch's narrative is exceedingly interesting, for, although his interpretation of the legend is typical of the mysticism of the Romanized cult of Isis which had little in common with its Egyptian original, nevertheless the legend itself varies very little from what is known about the older traditions and beliefs concerning Osiris.

Plutarch begins his narrative of the Osiris myth with an account, which is obviously Egyptian, of the legends connected with the god's birth. He then goes on to relate that Osiris became king over the Egyptians and taught them the arts of civilization. His brother Typhon, however, the god Set of the Egyptians, who seems to have typified the terror of the desert and the powers of evil generally, entered into a conspiracy with the queen of Ethiopia and seventy-two others against him. The queen secretly measured the body of Osiris and made a handsome and highly ornamented coffin to fit it. Osiris was then asked to a banquet and by stratagem induced to get into the coffin as it fitted none of the guests present. Immediately he had got inside the conspirators shut the lid, fastened it down with nails and poured molten lead over them. The coffin was carried down to the river and drifted out by the Tanitic mouth to the sea, whence it was finally borne on the waves to Byblos. Isis, the sister and wife of Osiris, on hearing the news was plunged in mourning. Her first care was to rear Anubis, the child of Osiris and Nephthys, and she then proceeded to search for Osiris whom she eventually traced to Byblos. The king of Byblos had meanwhile found the coffin and built it into his palace as a pillar supporting the roof, and his queen, who found Isis weeping and dejected, took her as a nurse to her child. Isis eventually obtained the coffin and took it back with her to Egypt, but, when she was visiting her son Horus at Buto, Typhon found it and hacked the corpse of Osiris into fourteen pieces and scattered them broadcast. Isis on discovering this journeyed from place to place in a bark of papyrus plants until she had found all the dismembered fragments of the god's body which by her knowledge of magic she was able to reconstitute and revivify. Osiris afterwards came from the shades to his son Horus, the latter undertaking with aid of the horse to vanquish Typhon, a task which was eventually accomplished in three battles, Isis having freed Typhon after the first. Isis after this gave birth to Harpokrates whose father was the dead Osiris.

Such, briefly, is the legend of Osiris in Roman times as told by a Greek with all the Greek love of fantasy and skill in telling a story. Although there is much in the narrative that is of Greek inspiration it follows the old native myths sufficiently closely for us to recognize that during the first century the same beliefs were current in Egypt about Osiris as for generations before. The legend as to the hacking in pieces of the god's body by Set probably originated in some dim recollection of the predynastic custom of dismembering the dead, but in Roman times all such traditions had long been lost, and the supposed fact that Osiris, with the aid of the magical powers of Isis, lived again in spite of dismemberment and became the father of Harpokrates after death merely intensified belief in his power over corruption and decay.

The cult of Osiris was something altogether apart from other religions of the time. He has been considered a corn-god[1] and a water-god[2], but his most remarkable attributes agree more with the theory that he was primarily a god of life-in-death. In him centred all the ideas connected with the springing up of new life from decay and corruption; he represented the

---

[1] *e.g.* by Frazer, *Adonis, Attis, Osiris.*

[2] Osiris as Nile-god seems to be confused with the real Nile-god Hapi-môû.

revivifying power in nature and particularly in man. We
hear little or nothing of what aid he afforded or good
he performed for the living, but for the dead he was at
once the hope, the protector and the judge. Slain and
cut to pieces by Set, by virtue of the magical knowledge
possessed by his sister Isis he had been revivified and
enabled to triumph over his enemy, henceforward ruling
in the underworld as king of the dead. Since he had
been victorious over death and was able to live again,
so also could man in the same manner conquer death.
In Osiris the Egyptian based his hope of reaching when
dead the "blessed fields," where the corn grew to a
prodigious height and the canals were always full; and
to Osiris he made his prayers for "royal offerings of
thousands of oxen, geese, clothes, and unguents," on
which his spirit might live for ever. Before, however,
he could reach the "blessed fields," he was led into the
judgment hall of Osiris, where his heart was weighed in
a balance against the emblem of justice and where he
made the so-called negative confession, in which he
declared that he had "not stolen, not slain man or
woman, not uttered falsehood" etc.[1] Osiris was at
once his judge and the pledge of his future existence.
Other gods and other magic might enable him to overcome the serpents and hostile demons that beset his
path to the "blessed fields," but in Osiris "lord of
eternity" lay his hope of living for ever. Before the
funeral the swathed and bandaged mummy was addressed as follows: "O thou who canst not move like
unto Osiris, O thou whose limbs cannot move like
unto those of Osiris! Let not thy limbs be without

[1] *Book of the Dead*, Chap. cxxv.

movement; let them not suffer corruption; let them not pass away; let them not decay; let them be fashioned for me as if I myself were Osiris": and the Rubric says: "If the deceased know this chapter he shall never suffer corruption in the underworld[1]."

In short the whole religion of Egypt was dominated by this veneration of a god by whose means the power of death was annihilated. In earlier times Osiris had only been one of several great gods of the dead, but at the end of the Ptolemaic period, so far as the populace were concerned, the other gods had disappeared or become absorbed in Osiris himself. Khenti-amentiu became identified with Osiris at a very early period. Upuaut had dropped out of favour long before Roman times, and the other two great gods of the dead, Sokari and Ptah of Memphis, had been united with Osiris under the triple name of Ptah-Sokari-Asar. Anubis, it is true, retained his individuality, but is nearly always represented in the subordinate position of embalmer of the body and conductor and herald of souls, an office which led him to be associated with Hermes Psycho-pompos by the Greeks. Osiris however not only occupied this supreme place among the gods of the dead but also played an important part as the principal deity of the triad Osiris, Isis and Horus. It was this triad that seized the imagination of the Greeks, and we can learn from Plutarch's elaboration of the Osiris myth how the whole legend was platonized for the benefit of the Graeco-Roman mystics. Osiris represented to them not so much a concrete example of a god living after death as the spirit of good, and at the

---

[1] *Book of the Dead*, Chap. xlv.

same time the male and productive side of nature. Isis on the other hand was the female and receptive spirit, and Set or Typhon typified aridity, barrenness, nothingness. Thus the whole legend became one of the struggle of Good against Evil. In spite of the temporary triumph of Evil, Good in the end is victorious. Osiris is slain but is reproduced again in the form of Harpokrates or the infant Horus. Thus, thought the Greeks, do the Egyptians understand and express the most profound mysteries in nature, the mysteries of Good and Evil, of Life and Death. It is however exceedingly doubtful whether even in Ptolemaic times the Eygptians had any such advanced conceptions concerning these deities. Their religion was always essentially concrete, and their mysticism was not philosophical but rather magical, seeking as its end the bringing about of a desired effect by means of concrete magic. The Egyptian legends, although they might lend themselves as a background to Greek Platonism, had in themselves very little in common with Greek metaphysics.

But if Osiris was in later times the principal god of the dead, the beliefs concerning the life in the underworld had been from the earliest period inextricably mingled with those of a solar system, probably of Asiatic origin, which was propagated by the Heliopolitan school of priests and centred round the sun-god Ra. According to this system the underworld, which was called the Duat (*Té*), was divided into twelve divisions corresponding to the twelve hours of the night and separated from one another by pylons. Each of these divisions was full of serpents and hostile demons. When the sun set

behind the hills of the western desert, after having
navigated the sky all day in his bark, he entered the
first hour of the night or the first division of the Duat.
His bark was towed through by different gods, and the
demons and serpents by which the Duat was inhabited
made fierce attempts to get into the bark and destroy
him.   As the boat advanced the sun-god grew weaker
and weaker until midnight or the central division was
reached, when the god was at his weakest and the
demons at their strongest.   From this point onwards
the sun-god grew stronger and stronger, the demons
weaker and their attack more feeble, until he burst
forth in all his splendour and strength from behind
the eastern mountains to recommence his voyage over
the sky.   According to this Heliopolitan system the
souls of the dead, instead of appearing before Osiris
and passing on, after judgment, to the "blessed fields"
which represented another Nile valley more full of
every material advantage, entered the bark of Ra at
night and were privileged to help keep off the attacks
of demons.   In the gloomy Duat they received strength
and light from the passage of the god, and when he
rose in the morning they greeted him with hymns of
praise.

These two schools of doctrine concerning the future
life became in very early times a source of much confusion both to priests and people.   The former made
some attempt to adapt them, giving prominence
naturally to the god or cycle of deities whom they
served, while the latter seems never to have evolved
any clearly distinct system and believed readily in one
or the other, or more often a jumble of both.   There is

little doubt however that Osiris, and Osiris only, was to all the god through whom immortality was to be gained, for since by certain magical ceremonies he had obtained immortality, so it was possible for man to imitate him. Ra the sun-god (and his various forms such as Khepri, Harmachis and Tum) was rather considered the beneficent deity in whose life-giving rays everything lived and moved and had its being. Every morning he arose in his pride and strength, causing all men to rejoice, and every evening he sank to pass through the twelve gloomy divisions of the Duat, temporarily delighting the shades who dwelt there with his presence. His rising again next morning was essential to the welfare of man, and the priests of Heliopolis every day went through a regular ritual to ensure it, for in the Duat was a serpent called Apepi, the arch-enemy of light and of the sun, and it was absolutely essential that the sun during the night should overcome this serpent fiend. Hence arose a kind of dual doctrine of Light and Darkness, resembling in some ways the legend of the fight between Osiris and Set. But whereas Ra overcame Apepi and his fiends every night and rose again next morning to rejoice Egypt, Osiris was overcome and slain by Set. Yet Osiris was able to overcome death and to make himself ruler in the underworld, thereby giving as it were a precedent to immortality. It was to Osiris therefore that the Egyptians looked as the god who could aid them to obtain immortality, although Ra was the beneficent giver of life to all things living and was as essential to man in this world.

Yet while these two systems continued to form the

outstanding elements of the Egyptian religion, of the vast pantheon of Egypt only a comparatively small number of gods retained general popularity at the close of the Ptolemaic era. It is true that in the great religious centres the veneration of the most obscure deities was not neglected by the priests, but the number of gods worshipped throughout Egypt had become much smaller. Many of the great local deities still retained their devotees in the districts where were their chief temples. Such were Ptah and Asar-hapi at Memphis, Sebek the crocodile god at Kom Ombo and in the Fayyûm, Hathor at Dendera, Horus at Edfu, Isis and Khnum at Philae, and even in the reign of Tiberius the Theban priests still boasted that Amonra was king of the gods. But a striking feature of this epoch is that certain deities seem to have become universal favourites, and after Osiris perhaps the two most venerated throughout Egypt were Isis and her son Horus or Harpokrates. Countless figures were made of these two. Isis is sometimes represented as Hathor, but much more frequently as nursing Harpokrates on her knees. Harpokrates appears very often by himself. But while the output of figures of the most important gods during the Saite and earlier Ptolemaic period was enormous, by Roman times it seems to have become confined almost to the above-mentioned trio and to the gods Anubis and Bes, the latter a grotesque creature, the god of music and dancing. These seem by the frequency of the images made of them to have found a place in the *lararia* of nearly every Egyptian at the time of the first Roman emperors, although when we turn to the funerary stelae and coffins we find a much more conservative type of representation, and many of the lesser known gods depicted. This is natural enough when we consider how conservative the Egyptians were with regard to everything connected with the cult of the dead, and also that the priests, who were better informed on theological matters, were usually the undertakers and funeral furnishers.

Alongside of this weakening of the national cults, Hellenic influence had begun to make itself felt, as in time it was bound to do, in spite of the jealousy with which the priests guarded the Egyptian religion and of the conservative nature of the Egyptians themselves. From the time of the earliest Greek settlers under the Saite kings down to the beginning of the Ptolemaic era, the Greek religion, although firmly established in certain of the Greek cities such as Naukratis, never made any impression on the Egyptians, and was looked on with contempt as the barbarian faith of a few foreigners. The Greeks on the other hand had always been willing to identify certain Egyptian gods with their own deities; for instance Ptah was thought to be Hephaistos, Amonra Zeus, Hathor Aphrodite, and so on. The Greeks however never properly understood the Egyptian ideas about these deities although they were quite willing to worship them, and there had never been anything approaching a fusion of the two religions. But after the Macedonian conquest the importance of Alexandria as a centre of Hellenic culture naturally made itself felt, though the process was a gradual one for the two reasons stated above, namely the power and jealousy of the priests and the geographical position of the city itself, away from the great centres of the native religion. Nevertheless Alexandria was a channel through which not only Hellenic but many other foreign religious influences slowly won their way into the Nile valley. For the religion of Alexandria was never purely Hellenic. Certainly all the Greek features were to be found, Greek gods and temples, and all the machinery of festivals and games, but from the very first the worship of all sorts of foreign deities began to be tolerated, including that of Adonis, Atys, Mithra, and Cybele, Syrian cults which later found their devotees throughout the length and breadth of the Roman empire. The presence also of a very large number of Jews, attracted by special advantages offered by Alexander and renewed by Ptolemy I, when the city was in its infancy, admitted the worship of Jehovah. This worship was not, however, entirely new to Egypt, for a large colony of Jews had settled under Darius in the immediate neighbourhood of the first cataract and had built a temple there, apparently becoming a prosperous and important colony[1]. But Judaism, being an intensely national creed, was practically confined to the Jews themselves. Other strange cults were introduced by wandering merchants and travellers, while it has even been supposed that the religion of Buddha was actively propagated in Alexandria. A rock tablet at Girnar in Gujerat, containing the edicts of Açoka grandson of Chandragupta

[1] This we know from the Aramaic papyri recently discovered at Elephantine. (See [Sachau, *Aramäische Papyrus und Ostraka aus Elephantine*, Leipzig, 1911, and *cf.*] Sayce and Cowley, *Aramaic Papyri*, 1906.)

(the Sandrakottos of the Greeks, a contemporary of Seleukos I), contains the following remarkable words: " And the Greek king (Yoni-raja) besides, by whom the Chapta (Egyptian) kings Ptolemaios and Gonkakenos (Antigonus Gonatas) have been induced to allow that both here and in foreign countries everywhere the people may follow the doctrine of the religion of Devanipya wheresoever it reacheth[1]." This throws a remarkable light on the intercourse between the subjects of the early Buddhist kings and those of the successors of Alexander, yet it is insufficient evidence on which to base a theory of Buddhist propaganda in the western Hellenic states, as has been attempted[2]. Besides the lack of all Greek testimony in an age when every form of religion was a subject of eager speculation, it is probable that the reading "Chapta" is very doubt-ful[3], which does away with the value of the evidence so far as Egypt is concerned. It is of course possible that there may have been a few followers of Gautama in the Indian caravans who taught their doctrines in the cities of the west, but it is impossible to conceive of their having been sufficiently numerous or energetic to have made any sensible impression on the religious tendencies of the time.

But unquestionably the most important deity in Alexandria was Serapis. The origin of the cult of this god is somewhat mysterious. For nearly a thousand years before the foundation of Alexandria an Egyptian

[1] Prinsep, *Indian Antiquities*, II. p. 20.

[2] King, *Gnostics and their Remains*, pp. 49 ff., 390.

[3] Wilson, *Indian Antiquities*, II. p. 23.

god known as Asar-Hapi[1] had been greatly venerated
in Egypt.   He was worshipped in the form of a living
bull which was thought to be the incarnation on earth
of the great god Osiris, and hence arose the double
name in Greek, "Serapis."   It would be natural therefore to suppose that the famous Alexandrine Serapis
was merely a hellenized form of the Egyptian god
Asar-Hapi or Osiris Apis.   Plutarch however (who, it
must be remembered, wrote towards the end of the
first century of our era, and whose evidence therefore
is some 350 years after the event) gives quite another
account of the origin of Serapis.   According to him[2],
Ptolemy Soter saw in a dream at Sinope in Pontus the
colossal figure of Pluto, who ordered him to bring the
divine image as soon as possible to Alexandria.   After
much difficulty he had the statue stolen from Sinope
and brought to Alexandria, whereupon Timotheus his
interpreter and Manetho of Sebennytus persuaded the
king that it was no other than Serapis, and after it
had been set up in Alexandria it got the name that
Pluto bore among the Egyptians, *i.e.* Serapis.   Tacitus[3],
Clement of Alexandria[4], and Cyril[5] relate the same
story but say nothing about the part played by
Manetho nor about the Greek equivalent of Serapis,
except that it was a god called Serapis that came from
Sinope.   Macrobius[6] adds that it was forced on the

---

[1] The origin of Asar-Hapi was due to the efforts of the priests of
Hapi or Apis at Memphis during the XVIIIth dynasty to raise their
god to the dignity of Osiris by declaring that their bull was the
incarnation of Osiris.

[2] *De Iside et Osiride*, xxviii.   [3] *Hist.* iv. 83.
[4] *Protrept.* iv. 28.   [5] *In Jul.* p. 13, ed. Spanheim.
[6] *Sat.* i. 7. 14.

Egyptians. In connection with this the shrewd conjecture of Letronne[1] is well worth recalling, which suggests that these stories were made up in later times by the Greeks, a people who always desired to ascribe everything to themselves, and who imagined that Serapis came from Sinope in Paphlagonia when as a matter of fact he really came from a mountain named Sinopion near Memphis[2]. The close proximity of Memphis to the Serapeum at Sakkara, where the sacred Apis bulls were buried from the time of the XVIIIth dynasty and onwards, lends considerable support to Letronne's theory. It is probable however that there is some truth in Plutarch's story. There is no doubt that Ptolemy Soter was anxious to find a divinity for Alexandria that could be worshipped alike by Greeks and Egyptians. He must have been informed that the cardinal doctrines of the Egyptian religion centred round the cult of the dead, and the god of the dead Osiris, who was also incarnate in the Apis bull, and thus Serapis was adopted as the most acceptable deity to become supreme god of Alexandria. On the other hand the Greeks might naturally object to a purely Egyptian god being given pre-eminence over the deities of Olympus, and accordingly the story was

[1] *Fragments d'Héron d'Alexandrie*, p. 210.

[2] This mountain is mentioned by Eustathius in *Dionys. Perieg.* v. 255. The name Σινώπιον represents the Egyptian *Se-n-Hapi* "place of Apis." See Brugsch, *Geographische Inschriften*, p. 240. [The theory of Lehmann-Haupt (in Roscher, *Lex. Myth.* Liefg. 61, pp. 338 ff.) that Serapis was of Babylonian origin seems extremely improbable. It ignores the Egyptian evidence and the Egyptian God Asar-Hapi.]

promulgated either at the time or soon after, that as
the new deity was a god of the dead he was really
Pluto, and it is easy to understand how, whether by
accident or design, the confusion of Sinope in Pontus
and Sinopion ("The Place of Apis") at Memphis was
made as to the place of his origin. It was for the same
reason, namely in order not to arouse Greek prejudice,
that the Alexandrine type of Serapis is never in the
least Egyptian, but compares more with the usual type
of Zeus, with curly locks and flowing beard, for it is not
likely that Greek taste would have sanctioned the
worship of a human mummy with a bull's head, which
was at that time the usual Egyptian representation of
Asar-Hapi. What the precise character of this god
was it is difficult to say, but apparently he represented
a sort of hellenized Osiris, an Osiris-Pluto, who bore a
name that would be acceptable to Greeks and Egyptians
alike. Not only did he become the paramount deity
in Alexandria, but later his devotees were to be found
in the most distant parts of the empire wherever the
Roman eagles penetrated. His temple was one of the
most magnificent buildings in the city, and its courts
were thronged with worshippers of every nationality.

As against these purely religious institutions of
Alexandria we must place the Library and Museum,
with its fellows and teachers of philosophy and rhetoric.
But this great university was little in touch with the
many-sided life of the city and still less with native
thought and feeling. Drawing their daily inspiration
from Homer, Plato, and all the glory that was Greece,
those who taught there thought themselves the apostles
of Hellenic culture, and felt little sympathy for anything

Egyptian, looking on the natives as mere barbarians. A few, like Chaeremon, may have paid some slight attention to the ancient civilization around them, but its meaning was closed to them by the barriers of race and prejudice, while the majority never learned more than the idle tales of the less instructed priests. On the other hand Greek philosophy was unintelligible to the Egyptian. Not only was his mind incapable of the reasoning and subtlety demanded by its study, but his language, which had never developed into the flexibility and pliancy of the tongues of Europe, was quite unequal to the task of expressing complicated and metaphysical ideas. Nevertheless, although the Museum had little effect on Egyptian manners, Alexandria herself had become the medium by which foreign ideas affected the old traditions of the Nile valley. At first, as we have seen, the process was slow, but the century and half that followed the incorporation of Egypt into the Roman empire saw a much more rapid disintegration not only of the old religion of Egypt, but even of the popular gods beloved by Egyptians and Alexandrians alike, Serapis, Isis, Osiris and Harpokrates. Also now a new faith was being propagated, for Christianity was launched into the religious vortex of the time.

CHAPTER II

THE EGYPTIAN RELIGION AT THE BEGINNING OF THE THIRD CENTURY

IF we now turn to the end of the second century of our era we shall find that the disintegration and decay described in the last chapter had become very much more rapid and marked. Although the priesthood still remained confined to a certain caste[1], and although it still prided itself on its knowledge of the religious mysteries over which it presided, there is no doubt that priests had become like people, practically conversant only with the garbled and distorted ideas which were all that remained of the great religious system of the past. Up to the reign of Decius, indeed (250 A.D.), a few priests still possessed some knowledge of hieroglyphics, but the proper writing of them had become a lost art some time before this. Even when Strabo at the beginning of the first century visited Heliopolis, the "philosophers" and "astronomers" were no longer there; all he met were merely "sacrificers and expounders to strangers[2]." This process of the gradual

---

[1] Erman and Krebs, *Aus den Papyrus der Kgl. Museen.*
[2] Strabo, XVII. 29.

dying out of learning among the priests had now been going on for two hundred years, and we find that the great majority of old Egyptian deities had become forgotten while hellenism had introduced new but bastard gods into the country, gods such as Antaios and Zeus Helios, while there even appears to have been a temple of Jupiter Capitolinus in the Fayyûm[1]. The art of Greece, too, had almost entirely replaced the old native style in iconography, although the funeral furniture of the period still maintained the older traditions. But the little hellenized terra-cotta figures of gods had completely ousted the bronze and faïence figures in native style of the Ptolemaic period. Harpokrates had become a fat, jolly Greek infant[2], now borne aloft on the shoulders of priests, now riding a goose or a lamb, or represented as dandled on his mother's knee. Isis wears the flowing robes of Demeter and is often only to be recognized by some small head-dress of feathers as being an Egyptian deity. Haroëris and Bes found great favour when represented as clad in the garb of Roman soldiers wearing the tunic and kilt and carrying the short Roman sword. Anubis frequently carries the *caduceus* and other symbols of Hermes. Even Osiris becomes altered, though less rarely, taking the form of Serapis or becoming round-bellied like the vases used to contain the entrails of the dead, in which

---

[1] Erman, *Egyptian Religion*, p. 224.

[2] Like Erôs, he wears his hair usually in the topknot, or the plait along the top of the head, characteristic of the small Greek boy; the long braided lock or side-plait of the Egyptian boy, which he always wears in old Egyptian representations, is sometimes added to his coiffure, and he often wears the Egyptian crown of Haroëris. The type was obviously confused with that of the Greek Erôs.

latter form he was called Canopus[1]. These debased types are interesting when we come to study the forms of early Christian iconography, for there is some probability that they were the forerunners of many well-known types in Christian art. The Madonna and child group was unconsciously inspired, in the first place, by the figures of Isis and Horus, while Haroëris, especially when mounted on horseback, is probably the ancestor of the military saints so dear to Coptic art[2].

Ignorance and confusion mark the funerary customs of the time to a considerably less degree. Osiris and Osiris only was still the great god of the dead, the god through whom immortality was to be obtained. We find him still accompanied by Isis and Nephthys while Anubis performs the last embalming rites and Thoth weighs the heart and enters up the result on his tablets. Nevertheless, hellenism here and there had gained such influence that we even find Osiris represented as Pluto and Thoth as Hermes Psychopompos carrying a key[3]. But whether native or hellenized the relatives of the dead man still believed in the efficacy of embalming, and, if rich, of spending large sums on funeral furniture. Among the wealthy the burials of the period fall into two divisions. The first, prevalent among the less hellenized, is much more conservative than the other. The coffins continue to have rounded covers, sometimes

---

[1] This type was directly derived from the old "Canopic" vases used to contain the entrails, which originally had stoppers in the form of genii supposed to protect the dead. One of these, Amset or Mesti, had a human head, and was evidently confused with Osiris.

[2] See further, p. 139.

[3] Berlin Museum, *Ausführliches Verzeichniss*, p. 356.

with posts at the four corners, and are decorated with
debased but conventional representations of the judgment scene and of the deceased in the presence of
certain gods of the dead, and for these it was still
possible to find a priest who could scrawl a few lines of
funeral formula in the ancient hieroglyphic characters ;
nevertheless, for the information of the relatives the
name of the deceased had to be added in demotic or
Greek. The mummy was usually plainly bandaged or
covered with rude cartonnage, the face gilded and a
bound prisoner painted on the sandals. In the second
class considerable changes had been introduced. The
cartonnages were painted in gay colours to represent
the every-day clothing of the deceased, while the face
was moulded in plaster slightly tilted forward, and
painted with a most horrible realism heightened by the
insertion of glass eyes. Gilded or painted chaplets
surround the head, and a wreath of plaster blooms is
often grasped in the hands. At this period the
mummies were frequently kept in the house for long
periods before burial, and the coffins were fitted with
removable sides in order that the relatives might show
their devotion by viewing the corpse within[1]. A third
type is peculiar to the Fayyûm[2], where Greek influence
had always been strong owing to its fertile fields having
been granted in the past by the Ptolemies to their
veteran Macedonians[3]. This type is much more artistic.

[1] *Aegypt. Zeitschrift*, xxxii. 56. Petrie, *Hawara*, p. 14 f.

[2] It appears to have been found at Panopolis also. See Schmidt,
Ä. Z. xxxiv. p. 81.

[3] Mahaffy, *Empire of the Ptolemies*, p. 178. *Petrie Papyri*, i. pp.
34 ff.

In place of the doll-like plaster face a portrait of the deceased was painted on *gesso* on a flat board and laid over the head. Some of these portraits reached a high degree of excellence, notably those found at Hawara, but, as far as we know, this custom did not survive long after the days of Hadrian[1].

In the case of the poor the funeral arrangements were much more simple. The body was coarsely embalmed and bandaged and then put on board ship to be taken as cargo to one of the nearest cemeteries. Round the neck was usually tied a wooden ticket with directions as to where the body was to be taken, as for instance "To be unladen in the harbour of Emmau," or "From Bompaë." In addition to this there was generally an inscription, sometimes in Greek, sometimes in demotic, sometimes in both, giving the name, occupation and age of the deceased. The demotic usually adds some religious formula such as "May his spirit live for ever in the presence of Osiris-Socharis the great god, lord of Abydos," or "May his spirit serve Osiris[2]," etc. The study of these tickets has yielded very interesting information as to intermingling of Greeks and Egyptians in the third century[3]. Religion was no barrier to this, for we have seen that the Greeks readily worshipped the Egyptian gods, and that the latter had become hellenized to suit the Greek population in spite of the

[1] Cecil Smith in *Hawara*, pp. 37 ff. See also Edgar, *Graeco-Egyptian Coffins, Masks and Portraits* (*Catalogue Gén. du Musée du Caire*, 1905), Introduction.

[2] Strzygowski, *Koptische Denkmäler. Catalogue Gén. du Musée du Caire*, Vienna, 1904.

[3] H. R. Hall, *P.S.B.A.* xxvii. pp. 13 ff. (*Greek Mummy-Tickets in the British Museum.*)

conservatism of the priesthood. Intermarriage must have taken place also, to a large extent. Out of two collections of these tickets the proportion of Greek names to Egyptian is one in four and one in three[1]. But Egyptian names were often borne by Greeks or people of Greek descent, and to base arguments on names alone is misleading. Nevertheless it may be fairly inferred that a quarter of the population of Egypt had by this time Greek, Syrian, or Italian blood in its veins, the foreign element being naturally strongest in the north, and among the smaller officials in the towns. The two nationalities, Greek and Egyptian, were beginning to settle down under the common master Rome, and although the religion and *Mischkultur* was but a debased mingling of the two civilizations, it nevertheless possessed an individuality of its own which left its stamp not only on the By-zantine art of a later period but also on Christianity, which was soon to displace the old religions.

In Alexandria also great changes had gradually been taking place. The scepticism as to the gods of Olympus had found a counterbalance in the syncretism of the later Platonists. There was a tendency among all those, who like Plutarch desired to steer a middle course between Atheism and Superstition, to regard the gods of the various nations as the manifestations of divine powers which were really identical. Serapis had from the first played a double rôle, half Hellenic, half Egyptian, and to these qualities were now added those of Helios and Zeus. But it is in the

---

[1] Hall, *loc. cit.*

Alexandrian cult of Isis and Osiris or Serapis[1] that we
see this tendency most strongly marked. Plutarch's
treatise on Isis and Osiris makes it plain that on a
foundation of Egyptian tradition there had been erected
a cult which had been made to conform entirely to
the ideas of the syncretistic Platonists. Osiris and Isis
have, according to this Alexandrian philosophy, become
great powers or *daemons*[2]. Osiris is the male Principle in nature, he is Moistness, the Nile, the productive
Power. He is also Reason, as opposed to Ignorance, and
the spirit of Good generally[3]. Isis, on the other hand,
is the female Principle in nature, the receptive Power
who carries out the will of the *Logos*, who receives
only the good and repels the bad, forming in her womb
Horus who is the "perceptible image of the sensible
world[4]." Typhon is aridity, emptiness, waste, un-reason[5].
The fight of Typhon or Set against Osiris and Isis
becomes only another form of the struggle between
Ahriman and Ahuramazda, of evil against good, of
ignorance against reason, of sterility against productive-
ness. In the end Set is not completely destroyed, but
like Ahriman can always continue to do harm although
finally Good must always triumph over Evil.

This Platonic exegesis of the Osiris and Isis legends
is not in the least Egyptian[6]. Plutarch and the devotees of the Graeco-Roman cult of Isis saw the Egyptian
religion through the distorted medium of Alexandria

[1] Osiris and Serapis, as gods of the dead, had become closely
identified at this time.

[2] *De Iside et Osiride*, § xxv.

[3] *Op. cit.* xxii., xxxiii., xlii.   [4] *Op. cit.* liii.

[5] *Op. cit.* xxxiii.

[6] See Scott-Moncrieff, *Journ. Hellen. Stud.* xxix. p. 82.

where this cult had grown up. Besides forcing the Egyptian legends into conformity with Platonic doctrines they were led astray by an insufficient knowledge of the native cults. The side of the Egyptian religion which was most typical of the Egyptian mind was the one that they understood least. All the gross and materialistic legends about Osiris, which had their origin in the primitive epoch of Egyptian history, were thought unworthy of belief or to be understood symbolically by the initiated. To all Greeks and foreigners the animal gods of Egypt were a sore stumbling-block and their worship was explained by the Platonists[1] to be either symbolical or utilitarian ; but as a matter of fact the Egyptians worshipped their animal deities without assigning any particular reason for it, as they had always worshipped them from the time that they were the local nome " totems " in the predynastic period. It was not in the least illogical or extraordinary to them that in one district the crocodile was venerated, that in another it was hated and hunted, that in one town sheep were eaten and in another considered sacred, or that the people of Oxyrhynchus who were fish-worshippers descended one day on the people of Cynopolis who were having a fish dinner, and sacrificed and ate all the latter's dogs, thereby causing a riot which led to the intervention of the Roman garrison[2]. This sort of fray, which was most likely of common occurrence, was inexplicable to foreigners and would have been still more so if they had realized that the various local priests probably instigated them. For, if we are to judge from the

---

[1] *De Iside et Osiride*, LXXII., LXXIV.   [2] *Op. cit.* LXXII.

attitude of Plutarch, it would seem as if the devotees of the Alexandrian cult of Isis thought the native priests were possessed of the same esoteric gnosis as themselves[1]. They were looked on as models of asceticism and ceremonial purity, because they largely abstained from eating flesh, shaved their heads, and wore only linen garments. That ceremonial purity, especially in later times, was connected with these priestly observances is to a certain extent true, but the climate of Egypt naturally bred an abstemious people, while the custom of shaving the head had been universal among adults of all classes from time immemorial, and linen had always been the most suitable and the most easily prepared material provided by the natural resources of the country. But the shaven head, the linen robe, and Oriental frugality passed into the Graeco-Roman cult of Isis and Osiris as the outward sign of the rigid asceticism demanded by Platonic idealism. Nevertheless the priests, as we have seen, were the very class who most resisted Hellenic influence, and even if the Egyptian language had been capable of expressing Greek metaphysics, which it was not, they would never have understood or adopted these ideas.

To Plutarch and his contemporaries Osiris also had assumed the properties of the Nile-god and of the Spirit of Moisture, the first of which led him to be associated with agriculture while the second connected him closely with Dionysos and the Eleusinian mysteries. Long before this Osiris had absorbed many of the attributes of the productive Nature-gods, but his association with the Nile is of peculiar interest and serves to show

[1] See *J.H.S.* xxix. p. 85.

how confused the Egyptian pantheon became even in
comparatively early times. As we have seen, during
the XVIIIth and XIXth dynasties the priests of Hapi or
Apis, the bull-god of Memphis, in order to gain greater
prestige for their deity declared that he was none other
than the living incarnation of Osiris, and from this
identification arose the double name Asar-Hapi, or, as it
was called later by the Greeks, Serapis. Once confused
with Hapi of Memphis it is easy to understand how he
became identified with Hapi[1] the Nile-god, and how
his priests naturally claimed for him the gratitude of
all those who profited by the fertilizing and beneficent
irrigation caused by the annual inundation. Thus in
late times Osiris became closely connected with the
rise of the Nile and agriculture, a fact which has led
Mr J. G. Frazer[2] to think him a corn-god and a Nature-
god akin to Attis and Adonis. In support of this view
Mr Frazer urges the custom of planting beds in the
shape of the god's figure from which corn or grass grew,
and of making models of him in corn and wax. But
both these customs were *funerary*, not agricultural; the
former was certainly a mere piece of sympathetic magic
done for the benefit of the dead person and expressive
of the revivification of life from death by the imagery
of seed sprouting from inanimate earth. In earlier
times Osiris had nothing whatever to do with corn or
agriculture, but was a dead god who lived again as king
among the shades. This idea was still the dominant

---

[1] Or Hapi-môû, "Hapi of the Waters," to distinguish him from
the other Hapi, the bull-god of Memphis, who was identified with
Osiris as "Serapis."

[2] *Adonis, Attis, Osiris*, pp. 268 ff.

one in Roman times as countless funerary inscriptions
show, but ill-informed Greeks and foreigners exaggerated
the agricultural attributes he had absorbed in later
times partly in order to suit their own philosophic
preconceptions, partly to complete the identification of
Osiris with Dionysos and the Spirit of Moisture[1]. In
this way the later syncretists were enabled to link up
Osiris with the Eleusinian mysteries, and it would
appear from Plutarch that the devotees of Dionysos
and Osiris underwent a common initiation[2].

When exactly this Greek platonized cult of Isis and
Osiris grew up it is hard to say. Certainly it had been
in existence for some time in Plutarch's day and had
already obtained great prestige among the Platonists
of Alexandria. Its origin was probably due to the
fusion of Greeks and Egyptians which began in middle
Ptolemaic times, but the cult soon diverged from the
native traditions and theology which inspired it at
first, and became a bastard off-shoot of the Egyptian
beliefs. Nevertheless its devotees fondly believed that
they were carrying on the worship of the gods of
Egypt in the ancient manner. They thought that the
native religion was obscured by layers of accretions and
superstitions which only made it fit for the uneducated

[1] The identification of the triad Osiris, Isis and Horus with
Dionysos, Demeter and Apollo seems to have taken place as early as
the fifth century B.C. See Lafaye, *Culte des divinités d'Alexandrie hors
de l'Égypte*, Chap. I. Foucart's theory that Osiris was the origin of
Dionysos (*Académie des Inscriptions*, Vol. XXV.) is untenable. Dionysos
was an Aryan god from Thrace (H. R. Hall, *Oldest Civilization of
Greece*, p. 239; Jane Harrison, *Prolegomena to the Study of Greek
Religion*, Chap. VIII.).

[2] *De Iside et Osiride*, XXXV.

and vulgar, while they alone held the key of the true
Egyptian faith. This was, of course, a total inversion
of the facts. The teeming crowds who flocked to
witness the ceremonies at Edfu or Philae were taking
part in celebrations which, even at the end of the
second century, recalled rituals which had their origins
in the first Egyptian dynasties. The ascetic devotees
of Isis and the philosophers of Alexandria who adopted
a shaven crown and white linen robes were members
of an artificial esoteric society that was called into being
by the mingling of Greek and Egyptian civilization.

This Graeco-Roman cult of Isis and Osiris reached
its culminating point at the end of the second century
of our era, but its great popularity was not confined to
Alexandria and the immediate neighbourhood. Temples
were erected to Isis, and, in conjunction with her, to
Osiris-Serapis and Horus at Rome[1], Beneventum,
Herculaneum, Pompeii and Athens[2], while traces of
their worship have been found in the uttermost parts
of the Roman empire near Cologne, and even in
distant Britain, wherever, in short, the Roman arms
penetrated. The ritual and belief of these esoteric
devotees are described to us by Apuleius[3]. He tells us
of a religious procession which he witnessed. After
the passage of buffoons and merry-makers

"the crowd of those who had been initiated in the divine
mysteries flowed past, men and women of every rank and every
age, luminous in the pure whiteness of their linen robes. The

[1] There had been a college of Isiac priests (*pastophori*) at Rome
since the time of Sulla. Apuleius, *Metamorphoses*, XI.

[2] See Lafaye, *Culte des divinités d'Alexandrie hors de l'Égypte*.

[3] [Schwabe in Pauly-Wissowa, *Real-Encyclopädie der class. Alt.*,
gives the date of Apuleius as *circa* 125 A.D.]

women wore a spotless covering wound round their moistened hair ; the men were completely shaved so that their heads shone again. Great stars of religion were they upon earth raising a shrill rattling noise with their *sistra* of bronze and silver and even gold. But after all came the prelates of the Mysteries, tall men with high girt linen robes, that clung closely to their form and fell about their very feet, bearing the emblematic spoils of the most mighty Gods. The first of these held up a lamp that shone with a clear light, not quite like those we use in the evening to light up our dinner tables, but a golden boat, holding a large flame at the point where its width was greatest[1]. The second was costumed in the same way, but he carried altars in both his hands, or *aids*[2], which derive the name they are known by from the providential aid afforded by the sublime Goddess. The third held a palm tree aloft as he marched, its leaves wrought subtly in gold, and he held a Mercury's caduceus as well. The fourth displayed an emblem of justice, an artificial left hand with its palm extended....The same man carried a golden bowl, rounded like a woman's breast, and made libations of milk with it. The fifth bore a golden corn-fan packed with small corn-shocks of gold. Another carried an amphora.

"Soon the Gods who have deigned to walk amongst us on human feet come forth; this one a monster displaying a long neck like a dog's[3], the other is the messenger of Upper and Lower Gods and shows a visage that is black on one side and golden on the other[4]. In his left hand he holds the caduceus, in his right he waves a green palm branch. A cow raised to an erect posture followed upon his traces. That was the emblem of the omni-parent Goddess Fecundity[5]. One of the blessed ministry bore it resting on his shoulders, gesticulating as he walked. A capacious chest of Mysteries was carried by another. It completely concealed the works of religious magnificence it contained.

"Another bore upon his happy breast the holy image of his Deity which resembled neither beast nor bird nor domestic animal nor even man himself. It was...an ineffable symbol of

---

[1] The solar bark of Ra with the flame symbolizing the Sun God.
[2] Perhaps small tables of offerings of the old Egyptian shape.
[3] Probably Anubis.
[4] Thoth?   [5] A strange survival of the goddess Hathor !

3—2

a religion that must surely be sublime and to be concealed in profound silence. In construction it was as follows. Its general shape was that of a small urn, most exquisitely carved out of shining gold, with a rounded bottom, and wonderfully chased over its surface with Egyptian emblems. Its mouth was raised to no great height and drawn out into a channel, which projected so far that it could hold a long stream of fluid. The handle that was fitted to it receded far in a swelling curve and upon it reposed an asp[1] in twisted coils, raising its swollen neck all furrowed with lines of scales[2]."

Apuleius also tells us how the goddess Isis appeared to him in a vision and told him who she was.

"My name is One," she said, "my appearance manifold. In various rites and under many names the whole world pays me homage. The Phrygians, first of the nations born on earth, call me the Mother of the Gods, under the title of Pessinuntica[3]. Those who sprung from the soil of Attica call me Cecropian Minerva. The Cypriote tossing on the waves invokes me as the Venus of Paphos : the Cretan archer as Diana of the Nets[4], the Sicilian, in triple form of speech, as Stygian Proserpina : the Eleusinians as the ancient Goddess Ceres : some as Juno, others as Bellona, others as Hecate : others again as Rhamnusia : the Ethiopians, the Aryans [sic][5] and Egyptians so famous for ancient lore who are all illumined by the morning rays of the infant Sun-God[6], and worship me with the rites that are properly my own, call me by my real name Queen Isis[7]."

The goddess is further described :—

"Her hair was a gentle flood that passed on each side of a neck that was divine, to extend itself at length in an ocean

---

[1] A serpent came in Roman times from being the general determinative of a deity to represent Osiris in particular.

[2] Apuleius, *Metamorphoses*, transl. Byrne, pp. 540–542.

[3] *i.e.* Cybele of Pessinus.   [4] Diktynna.

[5] [For the spelling "Aryans" Mr Byrne is responsible. The word should of course be "Arians," the people referred to being the *Arii* of the modern Afghanistan.]

[6] Harpokrates.   [7] Byrne's *Apuleius, loc. cit.* p. 533.

of swelling undulations. An elaborate crown of various flowers
bound her lofty brows, and showed in the centre of her forehead
a rounded surface like a mirror or image of the moon, which
radiated a soft bright light. Her temples right and left were
guarded by vipers that rose in curves, and by ears of wheat as
well, which slanted upwards. Many-coloured was her vestment,
woven of translucent silk, shining one moment in glistening
white, then yellow as the bloom of the crocus, and then again
blushing in flames of rose. But what gave confusion to my
regard wherever it chanced to meet it was her streaming pall of
irradiant, gleaming sable ; it circled round her form and rose
from her right side to repose on her left shoulder, where it was
held by a brooch, and falling partly downwards hung in a maze
of folds that flooded her lowest hem with the beauty of its knots
and fringes. Its woven border flashed with the same stars that
adorned it throughout, and a full moon breathed its glowing
flame in the midst. And wherever the glory of that *palla*
spread its flood, a garland, formed of all the flowers and fruits
that bloom, clung woven in its texture. Her emblems differed
greatly. Her right hand held a rattle[1] formed of bronze ; it was
a thin strip of metal curved round like a belt, with small rods
passing through from side to side, and when the three were
shaken by her quivering arm they gave a penetrating sound.
From her left hand hung a golden boat, and on the highest
portion of its handle rose an asp, raising its head on high, and
swelling a flattened neck. Her ambrosial feet were shod in
sandals woven in the palm leaves of victory[2]."

It is thus that Isis appears to the ecstatic Lucius in
Apuleius's tale, and it is easy to see how the goddess,
like the doctrine, had become completely hellenized.
Osiris, too, was called by his devotees

"God of Gods, who is the Mightier of the Great Ones, the Highest
of the Greater, the Greatest of the High, the Ruler of the
Greatest[3]."

[1] The sistrum.
[2] Byrne, *loc. cit.* pp. 531–532.
[3] *Op. cit.* p. 571.

Thus it is obvious that if the Egyptian religion had penetrated Alexandrian life and thought it had become completely transformed in the process. The Platonic syncretists had converted Osiris, Isis, Serapis and Harpokrates into great world-spirits, spirits who carried out the will of the Logos, and who demanded esoteric initiation and rigid asceticism from their worshippers, so that while the old native religion was crumbling away in the Nile valley it received a brief and artificial stimulus in its new environment of Alexandria.

But it was not only the Egyptian religion that was drawn into the meshes of Greek philosophy. The Jews had long formed a numerous and wealthy part of the community in Alexandria and their synagogues were to be found scattered all over the city[1]. They enjoyed the rights of *isopolity* and had their own senate and magistrates under a compatriot official called the "ethnarch" who was responsible to the Roman government, while the wealth and power obtained by their commercial activities gave them considerable political security[2]. But Hellenic influence soon began to make its mark on Jewish thought and literature, being noticeable as early as in the translation of the Hebrew scriptures into Greek known as the Septuagint[3]. In yielding, however, to the seductions of Greek wisdom the Jews found themselves in a different position to

[1] Philo, *De Leg. ad Caium*, § 20. There were also Samaritan communities in Egypt. See *Petrie Papyri*, II. 92, 93.

[2] They were attacked by Caligula for refusing to worship the Emperor, and a massacre of the Jews was also organized in the reign of Trajan.

[3] Gfrörer, *Urchristenthum*, II. 8–18. Bigg, *The Christian Platonists of Alexandria*, p. 4.

the syncretists of other religions, for it was impossible
for them to alter the Law in order to make it agree
with Platonic doctrines. Instead they calmly assumed
that the Law contained in itself all the seeds of Platonic
thought, and that an ancient translation had once
existed which must have been known to the earlier
Greek philosophers.

"By this means it was possible to argue that Plato was but
an 'Attic Moses,' and a swarm of treatises on Plagiarism solaced
the weaker brethren with ample proof that all the best sayings
of all the Greek philosophers were stolen from the Jew and
might lawfully be reclaimed[1]."

In this manner the doctrine of the Logos invaded
the Jewish religion, and it found its chief exponent in
Philo, the greatest of all Jewish philosophers. According
to Philo God is One, Eternal, and incomprehensible.

"God possesses not only intelligence but also reasoning
power, and using these powers He ever surveys everything that
He has created, allowing nothing to transgress its appointed
order[2]."

But God can have no name, as a name implies
limitations, and God is beyond all measurements and
limitations. Philo thus at times seems to transform
God into the "Eternal Negation of dialectics[3]," and
certainly pushes transcendentalism to its furthest limits.
The creation of the world and the relations of God to
man, are, according to Philo, under the direction of
certain Powers, resembling on the one hand the Jewish
angels who later became the principal spirits of the

---

[1] Bigg, *op. cit.* p. 6.

[2] Philo, *Quod Deus Immutabilis*, § 7.

[3] Philo, *op. cit.* § 5.   Bigg, *op. cit.* p. 9.

Kabbala, and on the other the Stoic *Logoi* and the Platonic *Ideas*. These Powers are under the super-intendence of two great Archangels, the one representing Goodness, the other Justice. The former and greater was understood to be meant in the Scriptures by the word *Elohim*, or God, the latter by *Yahweh*, Jehovah, or Lord. The sum of these Powers or Ideas or Angels is the Logos, the means by which and through which relations are maintained between the supreme Deity and the created world[1]. In this manner Greek philo-sophy was made the handmaid of the Law and also served as the medium for a considerable missionary spirit which hoped to prove to the Greeks and the more hellenized Egyptians the superiority of the faith of Israel over the pagan cults. But perhaps the most interesting result of this philosophic tendency in Judaism was the appearance of the "Therapeutae[2]," a Jewish community of men who bound themselves to for-sake the pleasures and distractions of the city life and to retire to the country there to lead lives of self-repression and meditation. The ideal established by this com-munity was thoroughly monastic, and it anticipated in many ways the monastic ordinances of Christendom. The Therapeutae retired each to his own cottage by the canals of the Delta or on the edge of the desert.

---

[1] For the philosophy of Philo see Siegfried, *Philo von Alexandria*, Jena, 1875.

[2] The whole of our knowledge concerning the Therapeutae is obtained from Philo's work, *de Vita Contemplativa*. The controversy as to whether Philo was really the author of this or whether it is a Christian work of the fourth century has been finally settled in favour of the Philonian authenticity by Conybeare in his admirable edition, *Philo about the Contemplative Life* (Oxford, 1895), pp. 258–358.

In their retreats they made it their rule of life to
watch and pray, imposing on themselves at the same
time vows of silence. They took as their motto "In
thy Law is my delight" and made the Mosaic Torah
their chief study. Their life was a purely spiritual one
divorced as far as possible from all fleshly desires and
considerations, the soul having to pass through a
novitiate of contemplation and "rationalization" before
"perfect good" could be enjoyed. This austere and
solitary life demanded that parents, country, wealth and
position should all be abandoned, wherefore it was
considered advisable that such renunciation should not
be made until practical experience had been gained of
every-day life, and not before the age of fifty was
reached. On this latter point Philo lays considerable
emphasis, which makes it seem that many of the rich
young Jews of Alexandria were led to premature
renunciation by their religious zeal. This ascetic ideal,
which had grown up under the influence of Platonism,
or at least of Greek thought, seems to have been widespread in Alexandria. Under its influence the Jews
turned from the pleasures and distractions of the life of
cities, and in communities, where each one dwelt apart,
pondered on the Law in the light of Greek philosophy.
These communities outwardly resembled those of the
Essenes, a peculiar ascetic society in Palestine, settled
near the Dead Sea, but the resemblance ceases when
the two are closely compared, for the intellectual and
philosophic movement which inspired the Egyptian
society is not apparent in the other. But not only the
Jewish religion, but also, as we have seen, the Egyptian
religion in Alexandria was affected in a similar manner

by Greek thought. Asceticism and probationary periods
of initiation were necessary for every true follower of
Isis and Serapis. Renunciation of the world and its
joys and cares was an ideal common to Jew and pagan
alike during the first two centuries, and the ideal
passed on afterwards into Christianity, which in its
turn introduced it into Europe, where it was modified
and finally transformed into the great orders of western
Christendom which wielded such immense power
throughout the Middle Ages.

These loftier aspirations find a gloomy background
in the superstition and practice of magic which was
indulged in not only by the Egyptians but also by all
classes in Alexandria. Egypt had always been renowned
for the skill of her magicians, and the fame of Egyptian
sorcery was spread far and wide. In truth the whole
of the Egyptian religion was based on it, and the great
funerary rituals, the " Book of the Dead," the " Book of
Pylons," the "Book of Breathings," etc. are in reality
nothing but compilations of magic formulae and
descriptions. The step from religious magic to " illegitimate " magic and sorcery was an easy one. Such
objects as the *cippi* of Horus and the *hypocephali* or
head-rests together with the countless magical papyri
show how universal the practice of magic and the use
of talismans were. The cippus[1] and the hypocephalus[2]
were most popular from the time of the XXVIth dynasty
to the middle of the Ptolemaic period, the former being

[1] The best example is the ''Metternichstele," published by Goléni-
scheff.

[2] There is a good example of the hypocephalus in the British
Museum, No. 37330.

a talisman pure and simple inscribed with invocations to Isis to protect the owner from all harm. Both of these objects, in order to be more mysterious and more effective, were covered with representations of the most extraordinary composite demons and pantheistic figures, the main design on the cippi being invariably a figure of Harpokrates trampling on a crocodile, symbolizing the victory of Osiris rejuvenescent over Set conquered, and this was deemed a most comprehensive phylactery against all forms of mischance and ill-luck. The pantheistic figures of these earlier talismans are of considerable interest, for in many cases they inspired the figures on the so-called Gnostic gems of the second and third centuries which represented the angels, aeons, principalities and powers invoked by the initiated to protect and save. The papyri also give us details of all kinds of sorcery and particularly of the " black arts," that is to say, the invoking of evil spirits to do harm to an adversary and the working of sympathetic magic by means such as the making of wax models in order to obtain the object desired[1]. The Egyptians not only practised these arts among themselves but introduced them wholesale among the Greeks and Jews of Alexandria and even into the capital of the empire itself. By the end of the second century, as a result of this, we find the Egyptians' gods mixed up in invocations with all sorts of deities and persons, as a few examples will show. In an address on a Greek papyrus of this period, conjuring up some potent deity, the following formula is used :

---

[1] See Budge, *Egyptian Magic*, pp. 94 ff.

"I call thee, the headless one, that didst create earth and
heaven, that didst create night and day, thee the creator of light
and darkness. Thou art Osoronnophris, whom no man hath
seen at any time ; thou art Iabas, thou art Iapos, thou hast
distinguished the just and the unjust, thou didst make male and
female, thou didst produce seeds and fruits, thou didst make
men to love one another and to hate one another. I am Moses
thy prophet....Listen to me ; I am an angel of Phapro Osoronnophris ; this is thy true name handed down to the prophets of
Israel. Listen to me, Thiao, Reibet, Atheleberseth. A...blatha,
Abeu, Eben, Phi, Khitasoë, Ib...thian, hear me and drive away
this spirit[1]."

Here we have the ancient Osiris Unnefer identified
with the God of the Hebrews and called by mystic
names very similar to those employed by the Gnostic
Christians. In another papyrus of the third century
Anubis is thus exorcized :

"Come in to me Anubis with thy fair face, I have come to
pray to thee. Woe, woe (?), fire, fire, [South, North], West, East,
every breeze of Amenti, let them come into being....For I am
Iae, Iao, Iaea, Iao, Sabaoth, Atone[2]."

In the same papyrus Set is invoked as follows:

"I invoke thee Typhon Set, I perform thy ceremonies of
divination, for I invoke thee by thy powerful name in words
which thou canst not refuse to hear : Io erbeth, Iapakerbeth,
Iobolkhoseth, Iopatathnax, Iosoro, Ioneboutosoualeth, Aktiophi,
Ereshkhigal[3], Neboposoaleth, Aberamenthoou, Lerthexanax,
Ethreluoth, Nemareba, Aemina, entirely come to me and
approach and strike down Him or Her with frost and fire[4]."

[1] Goodwin, *Publications of the Cambridge Antiquarian Society*,
1852, p. 7.

[2] Griffith and Thompson, *Magical Papyrus*, p. 75.

[3] This is none other than the old Sumerian goddess of the underworld. See *op. cit.* p. 61. The following name, Neboposoaleth, has
a distinctly Babylonian appearance.

[4] *Op. cit.* p. 147.

Again, a love charm contains this curious formula:

"I am the great Shaay who makes magic for the great
Triphis the lady of Koou. Lol Milol, the water of thy brother is
that which is in my mouth, the fat of Hathor worthy of love is
that which is in my heart; my heart yearns, my heart loves.
The longing such as a she cat feels for a male cat, a longing such
as a she wolf feels for a he wolf, a longing such as a bitch feels
for a dog, the longing which the god the son of Sopel felt for
Moses going to the hill of Ninaretos to offer water unto his god,
his lord, his Yaho, Sabaho, his Glemuramuse, Plerube....S. Mi,
Abrasax, Senklai; let N daughter of N feel it for N son of N; let
her feel a yearning, a love, a madness great....she seeking for him,
going to every place. The fury of Yaho, Sabaho, Horyo, Panto-
krator, Arbanthala, Thalo, Thalax: for I cast fury upon you of
the great gods of Egypt: fill your hands with flames and fire;
employ it, cast it on the heart of N daughter of N. Waste her
away thou demon, take her sleep, thou man of Amenti, etc.,
etc. [1]"

In this case we have the old Egyptian *shai* or spirit
of luck invoked, and it is common to find the word
used at this period generally for the *agathodaemon*[2].
Triphis is the goddess Tripe[3], and we have also the
ancient stellar deity Sopd mentioned. The rest has
a strong Jewish tinge. With the general decay and
intermingling of religions these various pantheons
were ransacked to aid the magician, and as the
old systems crumbled away before the advance of
Christianity the ancient gods dragged out the last
years of their existence as the hard-worked spirits
compelled to do the work of the sorcerer. Nevertheless the Egyptian of this late period not only depended
on magic and sorcery to obtain a great many of his

[1] *Op. cit.* p. 185.
[2] See Griffith, *Stories of the High Priests of Memphis*, p. 54.
[3] *Ta-rpet*, "the princess," a form of Hathor.

desires, but also took great pleasure in relating tales of
the prowess of the great magicians of the past such as
Iemhotep, Nectanebus, and Setne-Khaemuas, the son of
Rameses the Great and high priest of Memphis. The
tales[1] about the latter were very popular in Roman
Egypt, and those that have come down to us are certainly
among the finest fairy-tales of antiquity. An incident
in one of them shows this dark and superstitious side
of the Egyptian beliefs in a more favourable light.
Setne, or Setme, as he is called in this particular tale, is
represented as visiting the Tê (Hades), the old Egyptian
Duat, accompanied by his son Si-Osiri, and we are able
to glean from this story not only knowledge as to how
the old Egyptian beliefs about the future life lingered
on but also several interesting facts about the moral
ideas of the people towards the close of the first
century[2]. Before they set out for the mystic entrance
of the Duat, Setme and his son witnessed two funeral
processions.

"At a certain moment behold ! Setme heard the voice of
a wailing....and he looked from the upper chambers of his
dwelling, and behold he saw a rich man whom they were carrying
out to the desert necropolis, the wailing being loud exceedingly....
He gazed again, he looked, at his feet behold ! he saw a poor
man being carried out from Memphis to the cemetery....he being
wrapped in a mat, there being...and none walking after him.
Said Setme, ' By Ptah the great god, how much better it shall be
in Amenti for great men for whom they make glory with the voice
of wailing than for poor men whom they take to the desert
necropolis without glory of funeral !' But Si-Osiri said, ' There
shall be done unto thee in Amenti like that which shall be done

---

[1] Griffith, *Stories of the High Priests of Memphis*, Oxford, 1900.

[2] The date given by Griffith to the demotic papyrus containing this
tale; *loc. cit.* p. 41.

to this poor man in Amenti ; there shall not be done unto thee
that which shall be done to this rich man in Amenti.   Thou
shalt go into Amenti and thou shalt see....'"

Here follows a long lacuna in which it would
appear that Si-Osiri and his father go to the western
necropolis and gain the mysterious entry of the Duat,
or, as it is called in demotic script, the Tê.   When the
thread of the story can be taken up again, we find that
father and son have already passed through the first
three halls.

"They entered the fourth hall...And Setme saw some men
that were scattered and apart, they being also ravenous ; there
being others whose food, water, and bread were hung over them,
and they were hastening to take it down, but others dug pits at
their feet to prevent their reaching it.

"They entered the fifth hall, and behold ! Setme saw the noble
spirits standing in their places, and those who had charges of
violence standing at the entrance praying ; and one man in whose
right eye the bolt of the door of the fifth hall was fixed, he
praying, he uttering great lamentation.

"They entered the sixth hall, and behold ! Setme saw the gods
of the council of the dwellers in Amenti, standing in their places,
the attendants of Amenti standing and making proclamation.

"They entered the seventh hall, and behold ! Setme saw the
figure of Osiris the great god, seated upon his throne of fine gold,
and crowned with the *atef*-crown, Anubis the great god being on
his left and the great god Thoth on his right, and the gods of
the council of the dwellers in Amenti were standing to left and
right of him.   The balance was set in the midst before them,
and they were weighing the evil deeds against the good deeds,
the great god Thoth recording, and Anubis giving the word to
his colleague.   For he of whom it shall be found that his evil
deeds are more numerous than his good deeds is delivered to
Ama the Lord of Amenti, his soul and his body are destroyed
and she does not permit him to live again for ever.   But as for
him of whom it shall be found that his good deeds are more
numerous than his evil deeds, he is taken among the gods of the

council of the Lord of Amenti, his soul going to heaven with the
noble spirits. And he of whom it shall be found that his good
deeds are equal to his evil deeds, he is taken amongst the
excellent spirits that serve Sokari Osiris.

"And Setme saw there a great man clothed in raiment of
byssus, near to the place where Osiris was, he being of exceeding
high position. Setme marvelled at those things which he saw in
Amenti. And Si-Osiri walked out in front of him; and he said to
him, 'My father Setme, dost thou not see this great man who is
clothed in raiment of royal linen, standing near to the place in
which Osiris is? He is that poor man whom thou sawest being
carried out from Memphis with no man following him, wrapped
in a mat. He was brought to the Tê and his evil deeds were
weighed against his good deeds that he did upon earth; and it
was found that his good deeds were more numerous than his
evil deeds, considering the life destiny which Thoth had written
for him...considering his magnanimity upon earth. And it was
commanded before Osiris that the burial outfit of that rich man,
whom thou sawest carried forth from Memphis with great lauda-
tion, should be given to this same poor man, and that he should
be taken among the noble spirits as a man of God that follows
Sokaris Osiris, his place being near to the person of Osiris. But
that great man whom thou didst see, he was taken to the
Tê, his evil deeds were weighed against his good deeds, and his
evil deeds were found more numerous than his good deeds that
he did upon earth. It was commanded that he should be
requited in Amenti, and he is that man whom thou didst see
in whose right eye the pivot of the gate of Amenti was fixed,
shutting and opening upon it, and whose mouth was open in
great lamentation. By Osiris the great lord of Amenti, behold!
I spake to thee on earth saying, "There shall be done to thee
even as is done to this poor man; there shall not be done unto
thee that which is done to that great man," for I knew that
which would become of him[1].'"

This account of the visit to Amenti made by Setne-
Khaemuas and his son Si-Osiri is exceedingly interesting.
Although outwardly the Duat remains the same as

[1] Griffith, *loc. cit.* pp. 44–49.

ever with its halls or divisions, with its assessors, and with the scales under the charge of Thoth and Anubis, nevertheless the moral standpoint is considerably more advanced than would be expected, especially in a tale dealing for the most part with magical occurrences. It is true that in the past it had always been supposed that the deceased would have to deny a long series of crimes before he would be permitted to enter the realms of Osiris, but reliance was always placed a great deal more on a proper knowledge of the formulae and names of gods and localities required as a kind of passport for admission, while it was naturally the rich, buried with costly papyri containing all this information, who would be enabled the more easily to take their place " among the noble spirits." But in this Egyptian parallel to the story of Lazarus and Dives, we have a far higher moral enforced. It is not wealth and gorgeous funeral ceremonies that obtained " salvation " for the soul, but strictly the preponderance at the weighing in the scales of the good deeds over the evil ones. Again the division of the good from the evil is made on a different system from that in the past. The utterly wicked are still, as before, delivered over to Amit or Ama " the Eater of the dead," thereby meeting total annihilation. But there is an intermediate grade of those whose good deeds equal their evil deeds who are " taken amongst the excellent spirits that serve Sokari-Osiris." Yet another class of contemptible creatures is also mentioned, those who were helpless and shiftless on earth. Si-Osiri explains their destiny to his father as follows :

"These men that thou sawest scattered and apart, they being also ravenous, they are the kind of men on earth who are

under the curse of God and do work night and day for their
living, while moreover their women rob them and they find not
bread to eat. They came to Amenti : their evil deeds were
found to be more numerous than their good deeds ; and they
found that that which happened to them on earth happened to
them in Amenti—both to them and to those men whom thou
sawest, whose food, water and bread is hung over them, they
running while others dig a pit at their feet to prevent them
reaching it : they are the kind of men on earth whose life is
before them, but God diggeth a pit at their feet to prevent them
finding it. They came to Amenti and they found that that
which befell them on earth befell them again in Amenti, behold !
their souls were taken to the Tê. Find it at thy heart, my
father Setme, that he who is good upon earth they are good to
him in Amenti, while he that is evil they are evil to him. These
things are established, they shall not be changed for ever. The
things that thou sawest in the Tê in Memphis they happen in
the forty-two nomes in which are the assessors of Osiris the
great god whose seat is in Abydos[1]."

We are here able to recognize a sort of revolt
against the belief that the rich, buried with countless
ceremonies and costly provisions against hostile gods,
would fare more easily to the realms of Amenti than
the poor man unequipped with these advantages, and
also a reaction against the belief in annihilation for all
those who had not succeeded in qualifying by a
knowledge of the required formulae for a future
existence. The fate of the poor-spirited creature
unable to help himself is, however, as drastic as that
meted out to Tantalus. It is more than likely that
with the decay and waning influence of the priesthood
a fresh and more robust spirit was growing up among
the people. That the passages quoted above were
influenced by nascent Christianity is hardly likely.

[1] Griffith, *loc. cit.* p. 49 f.

The papyrus in question is not only of too early a date to admit of this being possible, but the major part of its contents dealing with the contests of the great magicians in the past would be the last kind to be influenced at all by the teaching of the gospels. Nevertheless a new spirit seems to have animated the dying faith of Egypt, and the growing ignorance about the countless rituals and formulae demanded by the priests in the past seems to have admitted this more robust conception of the future existence.

Incidentally such papyri as these show how the Alexandrian cult of Serapis and Isis had become utterly divorced from its native original. The philosophers who, with shaven crowns and linen robes, made themselves worthy to serve these two great spirits of the all-pervading *Logos* by contemplation and ascetic exercises have little in common with the native peasant, still imbued with the ideas of the past, still believing in the great judgment hall of Osiris where before the forty-two Assessors his soul would be weighed by Anubis and Thoth, and still with a very clear and definite idea of the realms of the dead and what would happen to him there. The difference is remarkable, and a comparison of the two works, the tales of Setne-Khaemuas and the treatise of Plutarch, must convince the most hardened believer in the Egyptian character of the latter, that the Alexandrian cult had been platonized out of all recognition from the native point of view. While the Egyptians still clung to their ancient beliefs the Greeks and hellenized Egyptians borrowed the ancient gods of Egypt as pegs whereon to hang their Platonic doctrines. Mysticism and magic were common to both, while the Jews, although disdaining the worship of idols, had been captivated by the fascinations of Greek thought, and had succumbed to the doctrine of the *Logos* with its attendant asceticism and mysticism. Thus the second century saw a great breaking up of the old religions, but from the Egyptian religion there survived not only the belief in a future existence after trial and judgment had been passed on the good and evil deeds done in life, but a belief that this existence was only to be obtained through Osiris, a god who had once been a king on earth, who had been slain by the Power of evil, but who had nevertheless overcome mortal corruption and lived again as ruler of the dead. From Greek philosophy there remained the conception of the *Logos*, bringing in its train the spirit of asceticism and mysticism, and these were potent forces in Egypt before the advent of Christianity and were bound to have not a little influence on the new religion as soon as it began to make its first converts.

CHAPTER III

THE BEGINNINGS OF CHRISTIANITY:
LITERARY EVIDENCE

WHEN and how Christianity was first introduced into Egypt is quite unknown. The tradition which makes Saint Mark the first preacher of the gospel in Alexandria is probably of the third century and has no historical foundation, although it was widely received after the first ages of the Church and continues to this day. Eusebius mentions it in his *Ecclesiastical History* but only as a traditional report[1], while the Alexandrian list of bishops from Mark downwards is quite an artificial production from which little or nothing can be learnt[2]. Nevertheless, about 180 A.D., when the Church in Alexandria first appears in the daylight of history, it is a flourishing institution with an organization and school of higher learning attached which must have already made its influence felt far beyond the city itself. Eusebius tells us that "thousands...were martyred from Egypt and all the Thebaïs" during the persecution of Septimius Severus in 202[3] A.D., and Clement writing at about the same

---

[1] *H. E.* ii. 16.
[2] Harnack, *Chronologie*, i. pp. 124 and 202 ff.
[3] *H. E.* vi. 1, 2 and 3.

date tells us that Christianity had spread to "every nation, village and town[1]."

Allowing for exaggeration on the part of Eusebius we see accordingly that while the pagan religious systems were undergoing the modification and decay described in the last two chapters Christianity had been making great strides. But the literary evidence is extremely scanty as to this period, while the archaeological is scattered and uncertain. One thing however is certain, viz., that all our evidence must be examined in the light of what has already been said about the changing and decaying religions which formed the environment of the new faith. If this be done it will be possible to account for some if not many of the peculiarities always presented by Egyptian Christianity.

Although neither Christian nor pagan literary evidence throws any light on the early days of the church in Alexandria, with the episcopate of Demetrius in 180 A.D. events become more clear. Unfortunately our chief author of this period, Clement of Alexandria, only gives us scanty and widely separated allusions to anything that may be said to be historical concerning the period that lay before his time, but if he tells us nothing about the early struggles of the first evangelists in Egypt, we are nevertheless able to glean from scattered references in his works some curious information as to the gospel they preached. In Clement's day it appears that besides the four canonical sources for the life and teaching of Christ, there were still in general use two other gospels, known as the Gospel

[1] *Stromateis*, vi. 18. 167.

according to the Hebrews and the Gospel according to the Egyptians[1]. There is every reason to suppose that these two documents preceded the four apostolic gospels and were in all probability there employed by the earliest Christian communities, for it is not likely that they would have forced themselves into popularity if the four sources bearing more authoritative names had been in the field from the first[2]. Clement however sharply distinguishes between these two gospels and the four canonical ones, and although they were apparently used side by side it is evident that the two earlier ones were beginning to be dropped by the more orthodox at the commencement of the third century. Nevertheless we are justified in supposing that up to the middle of the second century they were the principal if not the only sources from which the early communities learnt about the life and teaching of the Saviour, and their contents accordingly would be of the greatest interest and assistance in helping to an understanding of the motives underlying the development of the infant community. Our information on the subject however is entirely fragmentary. The Gospel according to the Hebrews was read chiefly by the Jewish converts, of whom there appears to have been a great number[3], either in Aramaic or in a Greek translation. Of its contents we know only scattered quotations, which nevertheless proclaim it to have had

[1] *Strom.* 2, 3, 9, 63, 93.

[2] So Harnack, *Chronologie der altchristlichen Literatur.*

[3] "It is perhaps a correct conjecture that more Jews were converted to Christianity in the Nile valley than anywhere else." Harnack, *Expansion of Christianity*, II. p. 305.

tendencies towards Ebionite doctrines in spite of its
close parallelism with canonical sources[1]. It purported
to be written by Saint Matthew, with whose gospel the
fragments seem closely related, but the name "according
to the Hebrews" arose from its having originally been
exclusively used by Hebrew converts[2]. It certainly
enjoyed the respect and even reverence of the early
Fathers, Origen and Clement of Alexandria[3].

The Gospel according to the Egyptians, again only
known to us by scattered fragments, possessed a more
pronounced tendency towards unorthodoxy, although it
was in use not only among actually heretical parties
within the Church but also by orthodox Christians, as
is plain from the attitude towards it of Clement of
Alexandria. Harnack is of opinion that the title implies
that it was in use originally among the Gentile Christians
of Egypt as distinguished from the Jewish converts[4].
Bardenhewer's view on the other hand is that it was a
gospel in vogue among the native Egyptians as distinct
from the Alexandrians[5]. For the latter opinion support
might be obtained from what we have set forth in the
former chapters : how different the native spirit was from
the Greek, and how in spite of the gradual spread of
Hellenism from Alexandria the native peculiarities in
religion, custom and speech still prevailed, especially
during the first two centuries. Alexandria had always

---

[1] The literature on this subject is enormous. A good bibliography
is given in Bardenhewer's *Geschichte der altkirchlichen Literatur*,
Vol. I. p. 383.

[2] Bardenhewer, *loc. cit.*

[3] See Nicholson, *Gospel according to the Hebrews*, p. 3 f.

[4] Harnack, *Expansion of Christianity*, II. p. 306.

[5] Bardenhewer, *op. cit.* p. 387.

been a foreign town to native Egypt, and the terms Alexandrian and Egyptian were in some ways anti-thetical[1], so that there is a probability of there having been a gospel suitable for native converts. Nevertheless there seems on the whole to have been little attempt at first on the part of the Christians to influence the *native* population, and the Gospel according to the Egyptians appears to have been strongly tinged with the philosophical ideas prevalent at the time in Alexandria among the Christians who were mainly of foreign descent, and to have advocated continence and asceticism as the duty of every Christian, admonitions which would closely coincide with the aspirations of both the Jewish Therapeutic communities and the ascetic worshippers of Isis. The fragments of this gospel that have come down to us are curiously enough all in the form of " Logia " or " Sayings " of the Lord ; those that are definitely from the Gospel of the Egyptians are the following :

I. The Lord said, " If ye be gathered together with me in my bosom and do not my commandments I will cast you forth and say to you, Depart from me, I know not whence you are ye doers of iniquity[2]."

II. The Lord saith, " Be ye as lambs in the midst of wolves." Peter answered and said to him, " If the wolves rend asunder the lambs ?" Jesus said unto Peter, "The lambs fear not the wolves after they die. And you, do you not fear them who slay you and have no power over you, but rather fear him who, after you are dead, hath authority over soul and body to cast you into hell fire[3]."

---

[1] Bardenhewer (*loc. cit.*) quotes in support of his conjecture the names of the two Macarii, one of whom was called the Egyptian, the other the Alexandrian. (Socrates, *H. E.* iv. 23.)

[2] Clement of Rome, 2nd Epistle, iv. 5.   [3] *ib.* v. 2.

III. The Lord saith in the Gospel, "If ye take not care of a little, who will give you much? For I say unto you, when there is faith in the least thing there is faith in much[1]."

IV. The Lord said to Salome, who asked how long death would prevail, "As long as ye women bear children. I have come to undo the work of woman." And Salome said, "Then have I done well in that I have not borne children." The Lord answered and said, "Eat every plant, but that which has bitterness eat not." When Salome asked when would be known the things about which he spake (i.e. the end of the world and the coming of the Kingdom of God) the Lord said, "Whenever ye put off the garment of shame, when the two become one and the male with the female, (there being) neither male nor female[2]."

V. And he said, "Him who confesses me, I will confess before my Father[3]."

VI. He saith, "Not everyone who sayeth to me Lord, Lord, shall be saved but he who doeth the will of my Father[4]."

VII. The Lord said, "My brethren are they who do the will of my Father[5]."

VIII. God (ὁ Θεὸς) saith, "It is not gracious of you if ye love those who love you, but rather gracious of you if ye love your enemies and them that hate you[6]."

From the evidence of Clement of Rome and other early writers it is clear that this Gospel according to the Egyptians cannot have come into existence later than the end of the first century. In general the Sayings quoted agree closely with the Synoptic Gospels, although they differ curiously in detail. Two of them however are remarkable, that is to say Nos. IV and VIII of the list. The first of these implies that our Lord enjoined abstinence from all sexual intercourse as a Christian ideal. This at once connects it with the early and once influential

[1] Clement of Rome, 2nd Epistle, viii. 5.

[2] As restored by Resch, *Agrapha* (*Texte und Untersuch. zur Gesch. der altchrist. Literatur*, xv, Leipzig, 1906), p. 252 f.

[3] Clement of Rome, 2nd Epistle, iii. 2.   [4] *ib.* iv. 2.

[5] *ib.* ix. 11.   [6] *ib.* xiii. 4.

sect of the Encratites, originally not a heretical sect
but a party within the Church, who set up a strictly
ascetic mode of life as the one most acceptable to the
Master. Encratism demanded abstinence from marriage
and all ties of affection, together with the refusal of
meat and wine as food and drink; moreover we know
that the Encratites continued to use the Gospel
according to the Egyptians after the Church had
dropped it. But Encratism is undoubtedly to be
linked further back with the pagan philosophical
doctrine that Matter is in itself Evil, and we have seen
how the asceticism which grew out of this doctrine was
prevalent at the period in Alexandria. Not only was
the frugality of the native Egyptian priests held up by
Plutarch as a shining example to the ascetic devotees
of the Graeco-Roman cult of Isis in Alexandria, but we
know from Apuleius how worshippers of the great
goddess had to qualify themselves for her favours by
rigid abstinence in food and manner of life[1]. Again
the Therapeutae were dominated by the same ascetic
motives although modified by the Jewish Law, while
all through the philosophic and religious thought of
the time runs this same idea that the higher life and
the initiation into heavenly mysteries are only to be
obtained by asceticism and abstinence. It is therefore
small wonder that Christianity was affected by it,
especially in Alexandria. But at the same time
Clement of Alexandria, who had himself no leanings
towards Encratism, defends this gospel from the
charge of extreme Encratism, a fact which shows that
it was only tinged with the prevalent doctrines of the

[1] *Metamorphoses*, XI.

time, although it seems likely that the preaching of
rigid asceticism was one of its elements. Nevertheless
it appears, from what may be judged of its general
tenor from the remaining Sayings, and from the fact
that it was still used by the orthodox in Clement's day,
to have had none of the more advanced theories
propagated by the extremer Encratists, which soon
developed into many of the fantastic ideas of the
various Gnostic sects. The second peculiarity to be
noticed is in Saying VIII, where the word God is used
where obviously Christ is intended to be speaking.
We have here a distinct indication of a tendency to
Modalism and the heresy of the Sabellians, who we know
appealed to this gospel for authority in support of their
doctrine that Father, Son and Spirit were one[1].

But a comparatively recent discovery has thrown a
flood of light on the early uncanonical gospels in use in
Egypt, a flood of light which, however, has only served
to intensify the shadows surrounding the whole subject.
In the year 1897 excavations made by Messrs Grenfell
and Hunt on the site of the ancient town of Oxyrhynchus,
about 120 miles south of Cairo, brought to light
amongst a host of papyrus fragments of all kinds and
of varying interest a page from a book, $15 \times 9·7$ centi-
metres in size, containing a number of Sayings of Jesus[2].
The finders dated this precious MS. on palaeographic
and other grounds between 150 A.D. as a *terminus a quo*
and 300 A.D. as a *terminus ad quem,* and more exactly
ascribed it probably to a date soon after 200. These
Sayings were as follows:

[1] Epiphanius, *Haer.* LXII. 2.
[2] Grenfell and Hunt, *Oxyrhynchus Papyri,* II.

I. "......and then shalt thou see clearly to cast out the mote that is in thy brother's eye."

II. Jesus said, "Except ye fast to the world, ye shall in no wise find the Kingdom of God ; and except ye make the sabbath a real sabbath, ye shall not see the Father."

III. Jesus saith, "I stood in the midst of the world and in the flesh was I seen of them, and I found all men drunken, and none found I athirst among them, and my soul grieveth over the sons of men, because they are blind in the heart and see not......

IV. ......poverty."

V. Jesus saith, "Wherever there are two, they are not without God, and wherever there is one alone, I say, I am with him. Raise the stone and there thou shalt find me ; cleave the wood and there am I."

VI. Jesus saith, "A prophet is not acceptable in his own country, neither does a physician work cures upon them that know him."

VII. Jesus saith, "A city built upon the top of a high hill and stablished can neither fall nor be hid."

VIII. Jesus saith, "Thou hearest with one ear, but the other thou hast closed."

This remarkable discovery was followed up in 1904 by the finding on the same site of a further series of Sayings closely related to the above but written not on the leaf of a book but on the back of a survey-list of various pieces of land ; it is dated by the finders as nearly contemporary with the first series[1]. The Sayings are as follows :

(Introduction.) These are the [wonderful ?] words which Jesus the living [Lord] spake to......and Thomas, and he said unto [them], "Every one that hearkens to these words shall never taste of death."

I. Jesus saith, "Let not him who seeks...cease until he finds, and when he finds he shall be astonished ; astonished he shall reach the Kingdom, and having reached the Kingdom he shall rest."

[1] Grenfell and Hunt, *Oxyrhynchus Papyri*, IV.

II.   Jesus saith, "[Ye ask ? who are those] that draw us [to the Kingdom, if] the Kingdom is in Heaven ?...the fowls of the air, and all beasts that are under the earth or upon the earth, and the fishes of the sea, [these are they which draw] you, and the Kingdom of Heaven is within you ; and whoever shall know himself shall find it.   [Strive therefore ?] to know yourselves, and ye shall be aware that ye are the sons of the [almighty ?] Father ; [and ?] ye shall know that ye are in [the city of God ?] and ye are [the city ?]."

III.   Jesus saith, "A man shall not hesitate...to ask...concerning his place [in the Kingdom.   Ye shall know] that many that are first shall be last, and the last first and [they shall have eternal life ?]."

IV.   Jesus saith, "Everything that is not before thy face and that which is hidden from thee shall be revealed to thee.   For there is nothing hidden which shall not be made manifest, nor buried which shall not be raised."

V.   His disciples question him and say, "How shall we fast and how shall we [pray ?]...and what [commandment] shall we keep ?...Jesus saith...do not...of truth...blessed is he."

It is at once obvious that these Sayings may be either a collection of traditional utterances of Christ or extracts from a lost gospel or gospels, but whether the former or latter, or what the latter were, and what relation they bore to the canonical versions, has been the source of endless dispute and argument among theologians.   When the first series was published the editors, Messrs Grenfell and Hunt, inclined to the belief that the fragment was a collection of Sayings of our Lord, that differed from all the known gospels, but contained little or no evidence to connect them with any particular sect or party in the Church[1].   Harnack[2] at once connected them with the Gospel according to the

[1] Grenfell and Hunt, *Sayings of Our Lord*, 1897.   Egypt Exploration Fund.

[2] *Expositor*, Nov., Dec. 1897.

Egyptians, a theory already tentatively suggested by the editors but afterwards abandoned by them. Zahn on the other hand considered that the Ebionite gospel was probably the source[1], and Batiffol the Gospel according to the Hebrews[2], while Dr Armitage Robinson pointed out many traces of the Sayings scattered about in the works of Clement of Alexandria[3], a fact which made it probable that Clement was acquainted with them. The discovery of the second series did not help much to modify or to throw more light on the various opinions expressed concerning the first. That the two are closely related is clear from the fact that the texts are in handwritings peculiar to about the same period and are from the same site, while there is no inherent discrepancy in the first series being written on leaves forming part of a book and the second being inscribed on the back of a land-survey, for the latter method of using up space for even valuable documents was common at the time. On the other hand it is remarkable that the second series is prefaced by an introduction which purports to represent that the Sayings were addressed to Thomas and perhaps another disciple.

It is beyond our present scope to go into all the various and conflicting opinions that have been expressed concerning these famous documents, but a *résumé* may be given of some of the more important issues involved and of the more likely solution of the difficulties connected with them. In the first place considerable doubt has

---

[1] *Theologisches Literaturblatt*, 1897.

[2] *Revue Biblique*, Vol. vi. pp. 501 ff.

[3] J. Armitage Robinson, *Expositor*, Dec. 1897.

been thrown by some, including Messrs Grenfell and Hunt, on the theory that the Sayings are extracts from any one gospel at all, but it is rather suggested that they are a collection of Sayings as such. Apart from the argument that each Logion is apparently without context, the introduction found at the head of the second series definitely describes what followed as a collection of Sayings supposed to have been made by our Lord to St Thomas and perhaps another disciple. The choice of St Thomas may only be a daring claim on the part of the editor, although such a claim would involve the probability that the Sayings were post-resurrectional, which is not at all apparent from the Sayings themselves. But the fact that the Sayings are arranged without context and prefaced in some cases by the historic present "Jesus saith," does not exclude the probability that they were taken from some continuous narrative or gospel and re-arranged as they stand. This is at least as likely as that they were scattered traditions of speeches strung together without any context. But if they are extracts from some lost gospel the question arises, from which? Here again opinion has been widely divided. The Gospel of St Thomas might at first sight seem a natural source, from the Introduction to the second series, but from what we know of the later versions of this Gospel it seems to have little in common with our Sayings, although Dr Taylor has ingeniously traced out certain parallels between it and the first series[1]. There was nevertheless an earlier form of Thomas's

[1] *The Oxyrhynchus Logia and the Apocryphal Gospels*, pp. 90 ff.

Gospel which was condemned by Hippolytus[1] as being quoted by the Naassenes in support of their ideas concerning the kingdom of heaven being within a man. But the quotation "He who seeks me will find me in children from seven years old; for there concealed I shall in the fourteenth aeon be made man" has but slight connexion with any of the Sayings[2]. Again the blank before the "and Thomas" in the second series presupposes another name, which would make the series the joint work of two evangelists, or imply that the first, so mentioned as being more important, was the sole author. Altogether the difficulties in the way of accepting the Gospel of St Thomas as the source are insurmountable, more especially since in its earlier form, as far as is known, this gospel dealt mainly with the childhood of Christ and possessed marked tendencies to extreme Gnosticism.

The case for the Gospel according to the Hebrews is much stronger since the discovery of the second series, of which the first Saying is quoted in part by Clement of Alexandria as coming from that Gospel. It may be recalled that the first Saying runs: "Jesus saith 'Let not him who seeks...cease until he finds, and when he finds he shall be astonished; astonished he shall reach the kingdom and having reached the kingdom he shall rest.'" Clement's quotation is: " as it is also written in the Gospel according to the Hebrews 'He that wonders shall reach the Kingdom, and having reached the Kingdom he shall

---

[1] Grenfell and Hunt however see here a close parallel with Logion II of the second series. See *New Sayings of Jesus*, p. 29.

[2] *Refut.* v. 7.

rest[1].'" Elsewhere he quotes the Saying in a fuller
and more accurate form without, however, giving the
source: "He who seeks shall not cease until he finds,
and when he finds he shall be astonished, and being
astonished he shall reach the Kingdom, and having
reached the Kingdom he shall rest[2]." There can therefore
be little doubt that this particular Saying at least had
its origin in the Gospel according to the Hebrews, but
it nevertheless still remains a moot point whether any
of the other Sayings either of the first or second series
have the same origin. The other chief arguments in
favour of this source are (1) the general Semitic construction of the sentences, and (2) the second Logion of the
first series: "Jesus saith 'Except ye fast to the world,
ye shall in no wise find the Kingdom of God, and
except ye make the sabbath a real sabbath ye shall not
see the Father.'" Apparent semitisms, however, are
insufficient evidence for a Jewish original, while it is
generally admitted that the latter phrase is to be taken
quite metaphorically and is in no way connected
with Jewish—still less with Ebionite—doctrines[3].

There remains the case for the Gospel according to
the Egyptians, which was brilliantly argued by Harnack
after the discovery of the first series[4]. We have seen
from what has been said before concerning the
fragments of this Gospel, that in spite of a singularly
close resemblance to the Synoptic versions, it possesses
traits of a markedly ascetic character. The conversa-
tion of our Lord with Salome indicates this very forcibly,

---

[1] *Stromateis*, II. 9, 45.   [2] *ib.* v. 14, 96.

[3] See, however, the arguments of Batiffol and Zahn.

[4] *Expositor*, 1897, pp. 321–340, 401–416.

while the reply to Peter's question in the second
quotation implies a strict and rigidly severe conception
of the relations between the Christian and the Judge of
mankind. Harnack is of opinion, moreover, that this
gospel followed in its Christology a higher spiritualizing
form more in harmony with St John than with the
Synoptists ; while he also quotes in support of the fact
that it probably had a tendency towards mystic modalism
a passage in Epiphanius which says that in this gospel
" all such [modalism] as if stowed away in a corner (ὡς
ἐν παραβύστῳ) is set forth mystically as coming from
the person of the Saviour[1]."   This, of course, seems to
imply that the reflections of the writer of this gospel
were put in the form of a " saying " of the Lord, of which
the dialogue between Christ and Salome is sufficient
illustration. Turning to the first series of Sayings he
goes on to point out that a very similar tendency is
evident in them also. Such phrases as "fasting to
the world" are distinctly symptomatic of Encratite
asceticism, while the judgment passed on mankind in
Logion III is rigorously severe. Again "raise the
stone and thou shalt find me ; cleave the wood and
there am I" and "make the sabbath a real sabbath "
are sayings which might well be interpreted " mystically" and were bound to lead to mystic and esoteric
conclusions. Finally, certain modalistic tendencies
of phraseology in the fifth Saying led Harnack to
write that it was "almost a precept of historical criticism : the new Sayings are extracts from the Gospel of
the Egyptians[2]." It might also be urged that they were
found in an up-country Egyptian town which was peopled

---

[1] *Expositor*, 1897, p. 408.   [2] *Op. cit.* p. 413.

mainly by native Egyptians with a large sprinkling
of people of Greek and Graeco-Egyptian descent.

To sum up. These Sayings are certainly from no
known canonical source, although in some ways closely
parallel to the Synoptic versions. Neither had they
any connexion with the Papian collection of the Lord's
sayings[1]. There is moreover nothing definitely gnostic
or grotesque about them, although they exhibit certain
tendencies to mysticism, while such phrases as for
instance are found in the second series "Strive (?)
to know yourselves, and ye shall be aware that ye are
the sons of the (almighty ?) Father" and "Everything
that is not before thy face and that which is hidden
from thee shall be revealed to thee. For there is
nothing hidden which shall not be made manifest, nor
buried which shall not be raised," show us where the
Gnostics found authority for their esoteric doctrines.
The Gospel of St Thomas, as we have seen, is an
unlikely source. It is true that the first Logion of the
second series is quoted by Clement as from the Gospel
according to the Hebrews, but there is nothing to
identify absolutely any of the other Sayings with this
source, while the whole trend of the first series is
towards the doctrine of the Gospel according to the
Egyptians as far as we know it. The learned editors,
Messrs Grenfell and Hunt, finally came to the conclusion
that none of these were suitable as a source for the
Sayings as a whole, and inclined to the belief that the
collection was a collection of Sayings as such, and that
the theory of extracts is unjustifiable[2]. But we have

[1] Harnack, *Expositor*, 1897, p. 402.
[2] Grenfell and Hunt, *New Sayings of Jesus*, 1904.

at least one clear case of an extract, namely the first
Logion of the second series which is undoubtedly from
the Gospel according to the Hebrews. It would seem
therefore that the Sayings were probably extracts each
prefaced by the solemn words "Jesus saith," but for
teaching purposes with all historical context omitted.
And the only likely sources seem to be the two gospels
most popular at the time, namely that of the Egyptians
and that of the Hebrews. It would be going too far
to suggest that the first series was extracted from the
former source and the second from the latter, although
there is no inherent improbability in it except that
there is a vague allusion to Thomas and another
disciple in the introduction to the second series.
Unless the theory of extracts is to be dropped
altogether, the only probable sources are the two
above-mentioned Gospels, one of which we know
for certain is quoted, while the other is closely
related in its doctrinal bearing. But with the
scanty evidence we possess it is impossible to assign
any particular Saying to either source, with the
exception, as we have seen, of Logion I in the second
series[1].

There were also found at Oxyrhynchus, at the same
time as the discovery of the second series of Sayings,
eight papyrus fragments containing a few lines of a
lost gospel, which were assigned by Messrs Grenfell
and Hunt to a period between 200 and 250 A.D.[2]
The fragment runs as follows.

[1] No attempt has been made to go into the question as to whether
any of these are genuine sayings of Christ himself.

[2] *Oxyrhynchus Papyri*, iv: *New Sayings of Jesus.*

" (Take no thought) from morning until even nor from even until morning, either for your food what ye shall eat, or for your raiment what ye shall put on. Ye are far better than the lilies which grow but spin not. Having one garment what do ye (lack?)...Who could add to your stature? He himself will give you your garment. His disciples say unto him, When wilt thou be manifest unto us and when shall we see thee? He saith, When ye shall be stripped and not be ashamed...?

"...He said, The Key of knowledge ye hid; ye entered not in yourselves and to them that were entering in ye opened not."

Here again we have a fragment of a gospel that was evidently very similar to the Synoptic gospels, and more especially to Luke. The chief interest however lies in the question of the disciples and its answer, both of which correspond closely to the dialogue of Christ and Salome in the Gospel according to the Egyptians. Unfortunately the papyrus is broken away after the word "ashamed" and there is no means of knowing whether the rest of the sentence corresponded to the "when ye trample upon the garment of shame; when the two become one, and the male with the female, there being neither male nor female" of the Clementine quotation from the Gospel according to the Egyptians. Again we have just enough to go on to be sure that this gospel must have been closely related both in doctrine and feeling to the Gospel of the Egyptians, but not enough for us to say definitely whether it is actually a part of that gospel or not. The editors are of the opinion that this fragment is not from the Egyptian gospel, nor is it the one quoted in the Clementine Epistle, as the wording and *mise en scène* of the Encratite dialogue differ[1]. It

[1] *New Sayings of Jesus*, p. 43.

shows however remarkably close agreement in being nearly related to the Synoptic sources and at the same time in being dominated by severe asceticism, not only with what we know of the Gospel according to the Egyptians but also with the other Sayings found at Oxyrhynchus.

In addition to these contemporary evidences of the early activity of the Christian communities in Egypt we have also the later Greek versions and Coptic translations of many of the works which we know to have been in circulation throughout the Church during the first two and a half centuries. Among these may be mentioned the manuscript found at Akhmim in a Christian grave of probably the eighth century and containing part of the apocryphal gospel of Peter in Greek. This work originated in all likelihood about the middle of the second century among the Docetist communities settled in Antioch, and was the subject of a communication by Serapion of Antioch to the Christians of Rhosus[1] about the year 200[2]. The Akhmim manuscript contains the account of the condemnation and passion of our Lord. Its most remarkable points are the statement that Herod was the judge who passed sentence, not Pilate ; that after the trial neither the Jews nor Herod would wash their hands, whereupon Pilate raised the sitting ; that Jesus cried out on the cross " My power, My power," and was then "taken up";

[1] About 25 miles N.W. of Antioch on the Syrian coast. The bishop's name "Serapion" may imply that he was an Alexandrian, but of course he was a Greek or Graeco-Egyptian educated in an entirely Hellenic environment.

[2] Eusebius, *H. E.* vi. 12, 2.

that the resurrection and ascension are put as taking
place on the same day; and that the first appearance
after the resurrection must have taken place on the
Lake of Genesareth. As to its value the opinions of
theologians vary, but it most probably represents a
later working up of materials found in the canonical
gospels in support of Docetist doctrine, while it also
presents a more exaggerated form of the tendency
towards exculpating Pilate and blaming the Jews
noticeable in the Gospel of St John and fully expressed
in the Acts of Pilate[1]. A Coptic fragment from the
same site, which is apparently to be dated as far
back as the fifth or even the fourth century, and is
undoubtedly a translation from an earlier Greek text,
contains what is perhaps another part of this gospel[2].
There are other Coptic fragments, now in the library at
Strassburg, which also contain a translation of an early
apocryphal gospel the original language of which was
undoubtedly Greek[3]. They contain a prayer addressed
by Christ to the Father and a description of the agony
in the garden and the ascension, and purport to have
been written by some or all of the apostles. The chief
peculiarities of this gospel are that in its phraseology
it possesses a markedly synoptic stamp, while its
Christology is of the higher spiritualizing type found in

[1] See Robinson and James, *The Gospel according to Peter and the
Revelation of Peter*. Harnack, *Bruchstücke des Evangeliums und der
Apokalypse des Petrus*.

[2] C. Schmidt, *Sitzungsberichte der k. preuss. Akad. der Wissenschaften zu Berlin*, 1895.

[3] A. Jacoby, *Ein neues Evangelienfragment*. As these fragments
were obtained through dealers in Cairo their *provenance* is unfortunately unknown.

St John. Nevertheless the human side of our Lord is
brought into strong relief by the fact that the saying
"The spirit is willing but the flesh is weak" follows
immediately after the words "The hour is come when
I shall be taken from you," and is not applied to the
sleeping apostles. Also throughout there is a general
tendency to mysticism but nothing definitely gnostic.
As is pointed out by Jacoby all these characteristics are
also found in the Gospel according to the Egyptians and
in the Sayings of Jesus for which reason he assigns these
fragments to the former work. Certainly they contain
similar tendencies, and unless there was a large number
of gospels circulating in Egypt during the second century
all tinged with the same ideas and alike in phraseology,
it is likely enough that these Strassburg fragments are
yet another part of this early evangel.

It is therefore quite clear from the evidence of these
papyri that the earliest sources of the life and teaching
of Christ current in Egypt were markedly influenced
by ideas prevalent in Alexandria at the time, and were
tinged with the asceticism and mysticism which were
the characteristics both of the Platonic Isiac cult and
of the Jewish Platonists. It next becomes a question
how these gospels were promulgated and how the
missionaries of the new faith were organized before the
episcopate of Demetrius and the rise of the catechetical
school in Alexandria.

There is no reason to suppose that the organization
of the Christian community in Alexandria during the
sub-apostolic age differed in any important degree from
that of the early church elsewhere. The offices of
presbyter and bishop were at first practically identical

and lower authority was delegated to the deacons.
Missionary work was undertaken by "apostles," a name
which was no longer confined to the Twelve. But an
interesting point that was never thoroughly realized
until the discovery of the now famous *Didache* or
"Teaching of the Twelve Apostles," is the important
position occupied by "prophets" among the early
Christians. This remarkable document contains, tacked
on to a work of Jewish origin called the Two Ways, a
brief exposition of the conduct meet for a Christian and
the manner in which those in authority in the Church
should be received. Its whole style and point of view
proclaim it as belonging to the earliest ages of the
Church. It is thus that the first Christians were exhorted to render due honour to those in authority.

"And as touching the apostles and prophets, according to
the decree of the gospel, so do ye. But let every apostle that
cometh unto you be received as the Lord. And he shall stay
one day, and if need be the next also, but if he stay three he is
a false prophet. And when the apostle goeth forth, let him take
nothing except bread until he reach his lodging, but if he ask
for money, he is a false prophet. And every prophet that speaks
in the spirit ye shall not try nor judge, for every sin shall be forgiven but this sin shall not be forgiven. But not everyone that
speaketh in the spirit is a prophet except he have the manners
of the Lord. By their manners then shall the false prophets be
known. And no prophet that orders a table in the spirit shall
eat of it, else he is a false prophet. And every prophets that
teacheth the truth if he doeth not what he teacheth is a false
prophet. But every approved true prophet, who doeth for an
earthly mystery of the church (*sic*), but teacheth not others to do
what he himself doeth, shall not be judged among you, for he hath
his judgment with God : for even so did the ancient prophets also.
But whosoever shall say in the spirit : Give me money or any
other thing, ye shall not hearken to him : but if he bid you give
for others that are in need let no man judge him. Let everyone

that cometh in the name of the Lord be received, and then,
when ye have proved him ye shall know, for ye shall have understanding [to distinguish] between the right hand and the left.
If he that cometh is a passer-by, succour him as far as ye can ;
but he shall not abide with you longer than two or three days
unless there be necessity. But if he be minded to settle among
you and be a craftsman, let him work and eat. But if he hath
no trade, according to your understanding provide that he shall
not live idle among you, being a Christian. But if he will not
do this he is a Christ-monger : of such men beware. But every
true prophet who is minded to settle among you is worthy of his
maintenance. Thou shalt take therefore all first fruits of the
produce of wine-press and threshing floor, of oxen and sheep, and
give them to the prophets ; for they are your high priests. But
if ye have no prophet give to the poor. If thou art making
bread take the first fruits and give according to the commandment. In like manner, when thou openest a jar of wine or oil,
take the first fruits and give to the prophets. And of money,
and raiment, and of every chattel take the first fruits as seemeth
thee good, and give according to the commandment......Elect for
yourselves bishops and deacons worthy of the Lord, men meek
and not covetous, and true and approved : for they also minister
unto you the ministry of the prophets and teachers. Therefore
despise them not : for these are they which are honoured of you
with the prophets and teachers[1]."

That this work is to be assigned to the earliest ages
of the Church is generally admitted by all theologians[2].
But if this be so it is curious that the writer seems un-
aware of the order of presbyters, although Schmiedel's
explanation of this, *i.e.* that in the particular locality
where it was written presbyters happened to be unknown, is perhaps acceptable[3]; and this locality might

[1] *The Doctrine of the Twelve Apostles*, ed. Bigg.

[2] The literature is very large. A good bibliography will be found
in Bardenhewer, *Geschichte der altkirchlichen Literatur*, 1902–3.
Dr Bigg is almost alone in assigning the work to a later age.

[3] Schmiedel, in *Encyclopaedia Biblica*, art. "*Ministry*."

with good probability have been Egypt[1]. In any case
the picture of the primitive Church presented to us by
the *Didache* is extremely interesting. Bishops and
deacons are only mentioned towards the end of the book
and the Christian is exhorted not to "despise" them,
from which it is evident that as yet they held little
position in the Church and were a comparatively
recent feature of the organization. The people who
play the important rôle are the "apostles" and more
especially the "prophets." The former are missionaries
who pass from place to place teaching and preaching
without being permitted to stop in one locality for
more than two days at a time, while the latter are
allowed to settle down or travel as they choose. Moreover in the celebration of the Eucharist the prophet
would appear to supersede all others, and is not
restricted to the set formula but may "give thanks as
he chooses." When he made utterance in ecstasy he
was above criticism, for to criticise was "sin against the
Holy Ghost"; and above all this "they are your high
priests" and received the first fruits of every kind. But
nevertheless there are warnings against (1) false prophets who may be detected by certain simple rules of
discrimination, and (2) prophets apparently genuine
whose utterances nevertheless are open to the gravest
suspicion; but these latter are not to be judged of men,
their "judgment is with God." It is therefore clear that
at the time when this work was written and in the
locality which inspired it, the position of "prophet"
was at its highest. Its authority was, nevertheless,

---

[1] Syria and Palestine have, however, been argued with equal
plausibility.

beginning to be shaken by the appearance of false and covetous prophets, men who used the office fraudulently as a cloak for vice and gain. Moreover we know from the *Shepherd of Hermas*[1] that many of these Christian prophets were nothing more than necromancers and practisers of magic and black arts, a fact which may perhaps explain how the grosser forms of gnosticism first became allied to Christianity, and may throw light on many of the irregular practices prevalent in out-of-the-way communities. The *Didache* at least shows us that already prophetic ecstasies were beginning to fall into disrepute, and that the struggle had begun between orderly organization as represented by the bishops and deacons and the irregular extemporaneous enthusiasm of the prophets which ended in triumphant victory for the former.

The *Didache* may represent what was general throughout the Church in the age immediately after the apostles, or, as is more likely, reflect only the organization of a restricted locality, but that it gives an indication of the manner in which authority was divided among the earliest communities everywhere there can be little doubt, more especially when we consider its relation to such works as the *Shepherd of Hermas* and *Second Peter*[2]. If it be possible to assign a locality to it, the most plausible seems to be Egypt, but it is out of the question to dogmatize where indications are so indefinite and vague. There seems however no

[1] *Mandates*, II.

[2] In this connexion see Schaff, *Teaching of the Twelve Apostles*. Armitage Robinson, *Encyclopaedia Biblica*, art. " *Prophetic Literature*."

insurmountable improbability that the picture portrayed in the *Didache* of missionaries and prophets, as the early teachers of the gospel, represents approximately the manner in which the new faith was spread in Alexandria and the upper country. If we place this period when the "prophets" reached the height of their power, and the organization of bishops and deacons had been generally effected, after the period of the *Shepherd of Hermas*[1], as is suggested by Harnack, it will be found to fit in very well with the years during which the various gospels were being preached with considerable activity in Egypt, and will also help to explain many of the difficult problems connected with this uncertain epoch. The *Didache* at least makes it more than mere conjecture that the first Christian missionaries or "apostles" went from town to town in Egypt never staying long in one place but always journeying hither and thither; some may have been "prophets" and have spoken in ecstasy, others plain men relating a simple gospel narrative. Here and there little communities would grow up among whom the chief part would be played by a "prophet" who would preside over the Agape or Eucharist and in ecstatic moments speak concerning the doctrines of the new religion "in the spirit." The gospels preached were probably not the canonical gospels, but such as the Gospel according to the Egyptians and the others which we have been considering. Owing to this ceaseless activity it was possible for Clement to say that "Christianity had spread to every village and town," and

[1] *i.e.* after *c.* 120 A.D.

Eusebius that the persecution of Septimius Severus involved countless victims[1].

It therefore becomes possible to draw certain conclusions from the results afforded us by what may be called the " literary " evidence. Dealing in the first place with the papyri and fragmentary gospels, it is beyond doubt that by the end of the second century Christianity had spread at least as far south as Oxyrhynchus and probably further.   Moreover the probability that the gospels first in use among the early communities were not the canonical ones is very strong. Clement of Alexandria in his writings displays full knowledge of the Gospels according to the Egyptians and according to the Hebrews, while at Oxyrhynchus there were in circulation " Sayings " of our Lord which contain a marked tendency to incorporate the ascetic and mystic philosophy of Alexandria with Christian doctrine, as well as at least one uncanonical gospel.   But both the Alexandrian literature and the Oxyrhynchus papyri point to the fact that, during the first two centuries of missionary effort at least, the appeal was made mainly if not entirely to those of Hellenic birth or education. As far as we know at present there was no attempt to translate any of the gospels or " Sayings " at that period into the native language so that they might be understood by the *fellahîn* population, who still worshipped the ancient gods of Egypt unaffected by Hellenic influences.   Knowledge of the new faith must have filtered through to these by means of those of their countrymen who had an acquaintance with both languages, and more probably than not in an imperfect or

[1] See above, p. 53 f.

distorted form. Also, although they might readily grasp the main points in the life and teaching of Christ they would little understand the mystic side except where it was portrayed more or less in a simply magical form, as was done by the Gnostic teachers. The spells and amulets of the latter would however find great favour with the native population.

When we turn to the manner in which the early missionaries preached the gospel we have less evidence to go on. Nevertheless there seems to be every reason to believe that, if the *Didache* does not present an absolutely accurate portrait of the state of affairs at the time, something very similar was taking place. The organization of bishop or presbyter and deacon was not effected until the " prophets " with their ecstatic utterances and the apostles or itinerant missionaries had obtained supreme power among the early communities. From the fact that not only the *Didache* but other early documents utter cautions against " false prophets " it is a fair conjecture that these prophets not only may have taught doctrines slightly tinged with mysticism and encratism, but have promulgated more definitely heretical creeds, and indeed have opened the door to gnosticism in its various forms. As there was no central authority, abuses would go on unchecked and the prophet escape condemnation owing to his sacrosanct office. In this manner the communities educated with some knowledge of hellenism would imbibe doctrines which if not actually gnostic were on the high road to gnosticism, and would appear, as far as we know from the success which the teachings of Valentinus and Basilides obtained, to have formed a fruitful soil for these esoteric

cults. The natives, however, who were still uninfluenced
by hellenism, and who probably only gained their knowledge of Christianity, as it were, second hand, would
probably be less affected by the philosophical side of
gnosticism and more by the magical.   Moreover even
after the formation of the catechetical school in Alexandria, there seems to have been little or no attempt to
influence the non-Hellenic community directly, such as
would permit it to carry on pagan practices alongside
of Christian worship, especially where the two seemed
to coincide. That this was the case can hardly be
doubted when we consider how conservative in religious
matters the Egyptians were, and the archaeological
evidence which will be discussed further on tends to
bear this out.

CHAPTER IV

THE BEGINNINGS OF CHRISTIANITY: FURTHER LITERARY AND DOCUMENTARY EVIDENCE

BESIDES the evidence contained in the last chapter there have been found among the papyri discovered in such numbers in Egypt during recent years not only two early prayers and a hymn of Christian origin but also several documents which offer very interesting material bearing indirectly on the early Christians in Egypt. We will deal first with fragments containing two early prayers and a hymn. The papyrus containing the first prayer quoted here is from Oxyrhynchus[1], that containing the second from the Fayyûm[2]. The phraseology of the first prayer presents no very marked peculiarities. According to Messrs Grenfell and Hunt it is to be attributed on palaeographical grounds to the latter part of the third century or the early part of the fourth. It runs as follows:

"O God Almighty who hast made heaven and earth and sea and all that is therein, help me, have mercy on me, wash away my sins and save me in this world and in the world to come through our Lord and Saviour Jesus Christ, through whom is the glory and the power for ever and ever. Amen."

[1] Grenfell and Hunt, *Oxyrhynchus Papyri*, III. pp. 12, 13.

[2] Bouriant, *Memoires de la mission archéologique française au Caire*, I. 1889, p. 243.

The phraseology of the second is somewhat peculiar and was evidently recited for another person. The text itself is noticeable for the fact that several words are accented or have breathings : it is written on the *verso* of a very early Coptic text. The prayer is as follows :

"I pray that the person named may not be led into falling, but to his salvation, but if he cannot hear that which is said for his salvation, may it be for a judgment. Jesus himself taught that his presence was for a judgment that those who see not might see and that those who see might become blind. The very word of the gospel taught that Jesus came not only for lifting up but also came for falling down : 'behold he is set for a falling and a rising up of many in Israel and to be a sign which is spoken against.' See that these words be not spoken for thy fall."

The chief characteristic of the foregoing seems to be a somewhat harsh and severe interpretation of two passages from the Gospels, *i.e.* Luke ii. 34 and John ix. 39. It appears in this way to be connected, as far as "tendency" is concerned, with the "Sayings of Jesus" found at Oxyrhynchus.

The hymn is written in metre, and the words are accented and divided perhaps with a view to the chanting. The translation here given follows the restorations of the editors Grenfell and Hunt, and of Wessely[1].

......that thou mayest receive life eternal
Thou hast escaped the hard law of the unjust.......
Thou hast come to the marriage of the king.......
Speak not in uncertain words without.......

[1] Grenfell and Hunt, *Amherst Papyri*, I. p. 23. Wessely, *Les plus anciens monuments du Christianisme*, p. 206.

Some come in sheep's clothing who are wolves within. [Ye shall know them] from afar.

Seek to live with the saints, seek to receive life, seek to escape the fire.

Hold to the hope thou hast learnt. The day which the master has appointed for thee is known to no man.

God has come bringing many things, having conquered death with a triple victory.......

Jesus suffered for this saying : I offer my back (to the stripes ?) that ye may not fall a prey to death.

The laws of God are glorious. He suffers as an example in all things that thou mayest receive glorious life.

He washed in Jordan, he washed as a type, he (Jesus) has the bath of cleansing.

He abode in the mountain and was tempted greatly by.......

Now thou art the inheritor. Now is the time now to give abundantly to the hungry.

God commanded to give food to strangers ; protect the strangers and the feeble that thou mayest escape the fire.

He whom the Father sent that he might suffer, who has received eternal life, who has received the power of immortality.

Tell the glad tidings unto children saying : the poor have received the Kingdom, the children are the inheritors.

He was scourged as an example that ye may have abundance in all things ; he has broken death so that it is destroyed.

That when thou art dead thou mayest see the resurrection, that thou mayest see the everlasting light, that thou mayest receive [the God of light ?].

Oh repose of the sorrowful ! oh cause of trembling to un-[believers] ! oh fire fearful to the wicked !

Thou hast come to grace without travail. Hear the prayers of the poor nor speak proudly.

Fearful is the fire, fearful to all eternity, fearful for the wicked. Christ......Christ is the crown of the saints, Christ is the fire for the wicked.

......singing psalms with the saints,......feed the soul evermore.

......forget not what thou hast learnt that thou mayest receive what he told thee.

Knowing these scriptures thou shal; never fear death.

Scanty though these remains may be of the prayers
and hymns of the early Christians, they show them
in a somewhat stern and unbending aspect. Let
us now turn to a weaker side of the new religion which
has been revealed to us by another class of papyri. In
the year 250 the emperor Decius broke the long calm
of toleration which the Christians had enjoyed since
the persecution of Severus. An edict was issued which
compelled all and sundry, men, women and children
alike, to sacrifice publicly to the gods, and commissions
were instituted in every village and town to see that
the edict was carried out. To those who were suspect
and who recanted, that is to say, sacrificed to the gods,
certificates of sacrifice were issued by the commissioners.
These certificates were called *libelli*, and those to whom
they were issued were called *libellatici*. Now the only
people who would be likely to object to sacrificing in
a formal way in public to the gods were the Christians.
As several of these *libelli* are extant, it is probable that
we have in them the actual documents possessed by
Christians who, in public at least, had recanted their
faith, and were certified by the commissioners as having
duly conformed to the pagan sacrifices. The *libelli*
follow a stereotyped form; at least the examples that
have come down to us all possess the same official
wording. It would appear from the papyri that the
forms were written out by official scribes with blanks
left for the names, which were in some cases filled in
with roughly and ill-written signatures[1]. The three
following examples came from the Fayyûm:

[1] Wessely, *Les plus anciens monuments du Christianisme*, p. 118.

"To the superintendents of the sacrifices, from Aurelius Kamis of the village of Philagris now dwelling in the village of Theadelpheia.

"It has always been my custom to sacrifice to the gods, and now, in your presence and according to the edicts, I have sacrificed and poured libations and tasted the offerings. Wherefore I pray you to certify. Fare you well.

"We Aurelius Serenus and Aurelius Hermas have seen you sacrifice.

"Year 1 of the Emperor Caesar Gaius Messius Quintus Trajanus Decius Pius Felix Augustus. Month of Pauni 21[1]."

Again :

"To the superintendents of the sacrifices of the village of Alexandrou Nesos from Aurelius Diogenes son of Satabous of the village of Alexandrou Nesos, aged about 72 years ; scar on his right eye.

"It has always been my custom to sacrifice to the gods, and now also in your presence and according to the edicts I have sacrificed, I have poured libations, I have tasted the offerings and I pray you certify. Fare you well. I Aurelius Diogenes have set it forth.

"I Aurelius Syrus certify that Diogenes sacrificed at the same time as we did.

"Year 1 of the Emperor Caesar Gaius Messius Quintus Trajanus Decius Pius Felix Augustus. Month of Epiphi 2[2]."

Again :

"To the superintendents of the sacrifices of the village of Philadelpheia from Aurelius Syrus and Pasbes his brother and Demetria and Serapias our wives, we living outside the boundaries. We have always been accustomed to sacrifice to the gods, and now also in your presence and according to the edicts we have poured libations and tasted the offerings. We accordingly pray you certify us. Fare you well. We Aurelius Syrus and Pasbes

[1] Wessely, loc. cit.

[2] Krebs, Sitzungsberichte der k. preuss. Akad., 1898, XLVIII. pp. 1007–1014.

have set it forth. I Isidore have written it for them because they are illiterate[1]."

The rest of this *libellus* is missing.

At Oxyrhynchus Messrs Grenfell and Hunt found another of these *libelli* couched in precisely similar language.

" To the superintendents of offerings and sacrifices at the city from Aurelius ...thion son of Theodorus and Pantonymis, of the said city.

" It has ever been my custom to make sacrifices and pour libations to the gods, and now also I have in your presence in accordance with the command poured libations and sacrificed and tasted the offerings together with my son Aurelius Dioscuros and my daughter Aurelia Lais. I therefore request you to certify my statement.

" The 1st year of the Emperor Caesar Gaius Messius Quintus Trajanus Decius Pius Felix Augustus.   Pauni 20[2]."

Yet a fifth *libellus* has been published which differs somewhat from the foregoing in that the certificate was apparently issued to a priestess of the god Petesouchos, a late form of Horus whose worship was prominent in the Fayyûm.   It runs as follows :

" To the superintendents of the sacrifices from Aurelia Ammonous Mystos priestess of Petesouchos the great god the great and eternal...[3]."

The rest follows in the usual official strain.   The fact, however, that this *libellus* was issued to a priestess of Petesouchos is important.   According to Breccia[4] it implies that certificates were issued to everybody and

---

[1] Wessely, *Sitzungsberichte de K. K. Akademie*, Wien, 1894, No. 1.

[2] Grenfell and Hunt, *Oxyrhynchus Papyri*, IV. pp. 49, 50.

[3] Breccia, *Bulletin de la Société Archéologique d'Alexandrie*, No. 9, 1907, pp. 88 ff.

[4] *Loc. cit.*

not to suspects only, for it is hardly likely that the priestess of a pagan deity would be suspected of being unwilling to comply with the edict. It may be admitted that in the general panic which the edict might cause, a good many pagans would secure *libelli* in order to be on the safe side, but it is hardly conceivable that every man, woman and child, including even priests and priestesses of the pagan cults, would become "libella-tici." If this were so, then the Christian origin of the other *libelli* would be extremely uncertain. Nevertheless we are confronted with the difficulty of the fact that in this particular case a priestess of Petesouchos had obtained a guarantee of "orthodoxy" from the commission. One possibility is that the sacrifice to the gods included sacrifice to the deified emperors of Rome, but this would not be objectionable to an Egyptian, still less to an Egyptian priestess, as the emperors received divine honours in all the principal temples in the same way as had their predecessors the Ptolemies and the native Pharaohs before them. Perhaps the conjecture of Botti is the best explanation, namely that Aurelia had originally been a priestess of Petesouchos, had been converted to Christianity[1] and under stress of persecution had sacrificed to the gods, taking shelter under her former title. In any case, whatever view we take of it, it seems scarcely credible that pagan priests or priestesses would find it necessary in the ordinary course of events to secure certificates of having

---

[1] Franchi de' Cavalieri, however (*Bulletin de la Société archéologique d'Alexandrie, loc. cit.*), thinks that the conversion of a pagan priestess in the third century is unusual. Why this should be so is not clear.

sacrificed, for they were the very people in whose
charge the sacrifices probably lay. Moreover the edict
was notoriously aimed at the Christians alone.

We have also clear evidence from other sources that
many Christians did obtain *libelli*. A letter of Cyprian's[1]
speaks of three classes of the feebler brethren who succumbed and sacrificed in the fear of martyrdom during
this persecution. The first consisted of those who had
burnt incense, the *thurificati*: the second of those who
had sacrificed, the *sacrificati*: and finally those who salved
their consciences by outwardly conforming to the edict
and obtaining *libelli*. These last were called *libellatici*.
Further it appears from Cyprian that it was possible
to obtain a *libellus* without taking active part in the
sacrifice either by touching or eating the polluting
offerings, and for this reason Cyprian would extend
greater clemency to the *libellatici* than to the *thurificati* and *sacrificati*, whose offence in the eyes of the
church was far more damnable. From all this it appears
that the edict was carried out in a somewhat perfunctory
manner, and it is easy to understand that, in the
Egyptian villages where notions of carrying out com-
mands were probably thoroughly oriental, Christians
with friends on the commission, or popular among
their fellow townsmen, might easily obtain a signed
and witnessed certificate without having to go through
any elaborate ordeal of actually sacrificing with their
own hands. The power of a well-placed bribe was
probably as great in Egypt then as it is now. Moreover,
if the Aurelius Syrus mentioned in libellus 2 and 3 be
one and the same person, *libellatici* were apparently

[1] Letter LV, Migne, *Patrologia Lat.* Tome IV.

allowed to bear witness to one another's orthodoxy. There seems to be little doubt that the edict was enforced in a typically oriental and casual manner.

We may conclude our examination of Christian papyri with a short notice of the epistolary remains. Of these the most important is the letter of Psenosiris which was found in the great Oasis of el-Kharga, probably at Kysis, the modern Dush el-Kal'a, with numerous other papyri, all of which dealt with the affairs of the guild of grave-diggers in that remote locality[1]. On palaeographical grounds the date of this papyrus is to be assigned to the latter part of the third century, but its contents leave little room for doubt that it is a document either of the time of the Decian persecution[2] in 250 or the persecution of Diocletian in 301. It is apparently a letter from one Christian "presbyter" to another announcing the deportation of a woman into the Oasis under the charge of some grave-diggers and commending the same to his correspondent's care. The letter runs as follows.

"From Psenosiris the presbyter to Apollo the presbyter his beloved brother in the Lord. Greeting.

"Before all I salute thee greatly and all the brethren in God who are with thee.

"I would have thee know, brother, that the grave-diggers have brought hither into the interior Politike who has been deported to the Oasis by the prefecture, and I have handed her over forthwith to the good and faithful among the grave-diggers until her son Neilos be come. And when he be come with God

---

[1] Grenfell and Hunt, *Greek Papyri, Second Series*, pp. 115 f. Deissmann, *The Epistle of Psenosiris*. Wessely, *Les plus anciens monuments du Christianisme*, pp. 125 ff.

[2] See Grenfell and Hunt, *loc. cit.* Deissmann, however, dates it later to the reign of Valerian, 257 A.D.

he will bear witness unto thee of all that they have done to her. Do thou also on thy part make known to me what thou desirest done here for I will gladly do it.

" I pray that thou mayest fare well in the Lord God.

"To the presbyter Apollo from Psenosiris the presbyter in the Lord."

The fact that this letter comes from Kysis and that it is the actual one sent, not a draft[1], makes it tolerably certain that the writer Psenosiris was then living in the great oasis and was commending his *protégée* to Apollo, another presbyter in the outlying district of Kysis, which lay on the desert route into Nubia and the south. With regard to the persons who figure in this letter we know nothing, they are merely names that flash forth momentarily through the darkness, conveying to us a glimpse of the troubles and adversity which afflicted the homes and every-day life of the Christians at that time. The name of the woman Politike we owe to Prof. Deissmann. The word in the text πολιτικὴν was originally given by Messrs Grenfell and Hunt the meaning of " harlot," a sense which it undoubtedly bore in Byzantine times. It occurs however as a proper name as well[2], oddly enough as that of a woman connected with the Roman cult of Osiris. Professor Deissmann has pointed out that not only was it unlikely for a public prostitute to be deported to

[1] Deissmann, *loc. cit.* p. 20.

[2] *C. I. L.* vi. No. 20616. On a marble urn :

D. M.

IVLIA POLITICE.
DOESE
OSIRIS
TOPSYCRON
HYDOR

See Deissman, *loc. cit.* p. 30.

the oasis but probably illegal as well, for only free men could be subject to the penal law of *relegatio,* and then only on the strength of an Imperial edict. Whether Politike was deported because of her Christianity or for some other reason is not certain, but there can be little doubt that she was a woman of the better class. It is also probable that the two presbyters were also refugees or exiles. Professor Deissmann assumes that the good style and knowledge of the conventional ecclesiastical abbreviations in writing, shown in the letter, imply that Christianity must have been well known for some time in the oasis. But it is more likely that Psenosiris and Apollo were themselves exiles from Egypt. Even the "faithful grave-diggers" need not necessarily have been Christians. Indeed Apollo, Psenosiris and Politike as refugees may have been the only Christians in the oasis, especially if the earlier date of the Decian era be accepted. At that time there would hardly be any organized Christian community in so remote a locality.

The whole phraseology of the epistle, however, is convincingly in favour of a Christian origin. The phrases " brother in the Lord," " brethren who are with thee in God," "in the Lord God" etc., make this perfectly evident. It is true that the name Jesus or Christ does not appear but it must be borne in mind that the letter was written when persecution was being applied to the Christians, and all the pious phrases would necessarily have to be of a non-committal character. In the event of the letter being seized, it would have been possible for Psenosiris or Apollo to plead that the word " Lord " referred to Serapis or some other god, as such phraseology was

current at the time[1], and as there would be no definite
evidence of any reference to Jesus or Christ they
would probably have escaped punishment. The same
applies to the word "presbyter," which may also be
construed simply the "elder[2]." Nevertheless taken
all together the phraseology is such as would never
have been found in a purely pagan document, and is
obviously the work of a Christian designing to write
a Christian letter without committing himself to anything definite which, in the case of the letter falling
into hostile hands, could be used as evidence against him.
The part played by the grave-diggers is interesting.
It is evident that some of them were either themselves Christians or at least well disposed towards the
Christians[3]. They were at any rate to be trusted with
making the journey of the unfortunate lady accustomed
to the luxury and comfort of Egypt less unendurable
and dangerous than it might otherwise have been.
They would be in any case strong allies for the
Christians to have, for not only have the papyri relating
to their guild at Kysis revealed them as an important
body, but the attention paid by all Egyptians, Christian
and pagan alike, to burial rites and mummification of

[1] "Our Lord Serapis" was a favourite expression.

[2] In Ptolemaic times it had both a priestly and official meaning.

[3] Dieterich's comparison (*Göttingische Gelehrte Anzeigen*, 1903,
CLXV. p. 550) of this letter with another from the archives of the
guild of grave-diggers at Kysis, which is remarkably similar in
phraseology, in favour of a pagan origin for both, is not very
convincing. No. 77 (Grenfell and Hunt, *Greek Papyri, Second Series*),
quoted by him, refers to the transfer of a *corpse* to the oasis not a
living person, nor does it contain the mention of the words "Lord" or
"God." His interpretation has been well criticized by Wessely, *Les
plus anciens monuments*, pp. 129 ff.

the dead, would give them a semi-sacred position. That
the oasis was used as a place of banishment for civil
offences[1] as well for Christian non-jurors is also known,
while during the Arian controversy the Arian bishop of
Alexandria, George, found it a convenient place to which
to send several of his orthodox opponents[2]. It is certain
that in this document we have the oldest extant original
holograph Christian letter that has yet come down to us.

With regard to the later persecution under Diocletian, when we know from Eusebius that Christians
were transported in batches to work in the mines,
Wessely quotes[3] two very interesting letters which, if
they do not actually refer to Christians, throw a good
deal of light on the methods of deportation and forced
work in the mines and quarries. The first of these
documents is a letter guaranteeing the work of certain
deported wretches and runs as follows :

" To ......khos who is also named Basianos, *praepositus* of
such and such of the Hermopolitan nome, from Apollo son of
Pekysis whose mother was so and so, the police officer of the
village of Pake of the Hermopolitan nome.

" I swear by the fortune of our emperors and Caesars to
guarantee the arrival on the 25th of February of the 6 workers
from this village hereunder described sent to the mines near
Maximianopolis, and to hand them over to those in charge of the
mines until March 7th.　They are :—

.... son of Belles,			age 25.
,,	,,	,,	age 30.
,,	,,	,,	age 23.
,,	,,	,,	age 30.
,,	,,	,,	age 20.
,,	,,	,,	age 22.

[1] Ulpian, *Digesta*, xlviii. xxii. 7.

[2] Socrates, *E.H.* ii. 28.

[3] *Les plus anciens monuments du Christianisme*, pp. 132–135.

"I guarantee that these persons shall fulfil their tasks thoroughly and shall remain.........until their exchange."

The second of these letters was written July—August 301, that is to say about the same period as the first. It is as follows:

"To Aurelius Origines prefect of the Hermopolitan nome from Aurelius Paësios son of Stephanos whose mother......and Silvanus whose mother was Helen, both being mayors of the village of Senombo.

"We set it forth and announce that the workers hereinunder inscribed who have been despatched to the mines of Alabastrine to replace those who have been deported there are in good condition and capable—this on our own responsibility and the co-responsibility of all the villagers. They are :—

Aurelius Entis son of Silvanus.
Aurelius ...... son of Tasytis.

"We make ourselves responsible for these and will answer for their thoroughly fulfilling the duties with which they are charged and that they shall not quit those who are already there until the order comes for their exchange. But if they are behindhand and we do not make due arrangements we ourselves undertake responsibility on their behalf and will confess if we are questioned. Year 18 also year 17 of our lords Diocletianus and Maximianus Augusti and year 9 of our excellent lords Constantius and Maximianus. In the 2nd consulate of Flavius Postumius Titianus and of Verus (?) Nepotianus. Month of Mésore. We have set it forth. I Aurelius Orion have written it for them for they pretend not to know how to write[1]."

It is thus evident that the imperial persecutions threw unenviable responsibilities on the local officials and village notables. Egypt changes little, and doubtless fifty years ago scores of similar letters were written by unfortunate *omdehs* who had to guarantee a supply of men from their villages for the *corvée*.

[1] See also Vitelli, *Papiri Greco-egizi*, Vol. i. pp. 16, 17.

Another letter of considerable interest found in the Fayyûm and published by Messrs Grenfell and Hunt is evidently part of a Christian correspondence[1]. Unfortunately the papyrus is in a very bad condition and the text is in many places obscure. On palaeographical grounds the letter is to be attributed to the third century. The main gist of the epistle is that a Christian living in Rome desired to travel to Alexandria and wrote to his friends in the Fayyûm with regard to despatching certain moneys due to him to enable him to make the voyage. The whole letter is apparently taken up with this monetary transaction in which the writer was deeply engrossed. It mentions however the πάπαι Maximus and Theonas, who have been identified by Harnack as Maximus the bishop of Alexandria 265—281 and Theonas his successor[2]. The papyrus also bears in later hands chapter i. v. 1 of the Epistle to the Hebrews and Genesis chapter i. vv. 1—5 both according to the Septuagint and according to the version of Aquila.

The last letter of this early period of Egyptian Christianity brings us down to the beginning of the fourth century. It is the epistle of one Justin to his friend Papnouthios (the Greek form of the Egyptian name Papnoute) and runs as follows:

"...to write concerning thy excellence, my dear lord. For we believe that thy citizenship is in heaven; wherefore we regard thee as our master and common protector. But lest I write and talk too much (for in much talk there is no escape from sin) I pray thee, Master, recall me in thy holy prayers that we may be partakers in the cleansing of sins. For I am of

---

[1] *Amherst Papyri*, I. pp. 28–30.

[2] *Sitzungsberichte der k. preuss. Akad.*, Berlin, 1900, pp. 984 ff.

those that sin. I pray you deign to accept this little quantity
of oil by our brother Macarius. Many greetings I send to all
our brethren in the Lord and may the divine providence protect
you long in Jesus Christ, beloved lord.

"[To my lord] and dear brother Papnouthios "Christophoros"
from Justin[1]."

It may thus be seen that the papyri found by
archaeologists in Egypt, although as yet few in number
and varying in value, form an important addition to our
knowledge of early Christianity and will have to be taken
into serious account by the ecclesiastical historian of the
future. In a former chapter we have considered the theological interest aroused by the discovery of the fragments
of lost gospels and the "Sayings of Jesus." The last
letter but one quoted above, the letter from Rome to the
Fayyûm, shows active inter-communication between
Christians separated from one another by long distances,
although this of course is nothing extraordinary in itself.
The evidence of the *libelli* is of first class importance,
for although they may not be the actual certificates of
recanting Christians, they are at least interesting examples of the methods employed by the emperor Decius,
distracted by the growth of a new-fangled and from
the Roman point of view anti-social religion, to force
conformity upon his subjects. The epistle of Psenosiris
gives us a glimpse of the deprivations endured by the
Christians under persecution, but it must be at the
same time admitted that these persecutions were

[1 "Christophoros" in this letter probably means that Papnouthios
was a bishop. The title "Christ-bearer" was commonly given to
bishops in the Coptic period (see H. R. Hall, *Coptic and Greek Texts
of the Christian Period in the British Museum*, pp. 55, 70, 98) and may
quite well have been used in earlier days.]

intermittent, and, if we are to judge by the *libelli*, under Decius were carried out in a very easy-going manner. The other fragments quoted in this chapter may not be of first class importance, but at the same time they assist in showing us the spirit of the age and to some extent the spirit of the early Christians in Egypt. One thing at least all the papyrological evidence tends to prove; that is, that up to the end of the third century the vehicle of the new religion was Greek, and that although there may have been many non-Greek speaking native converts, Greek ideas and Greek education, tinged perhaps with native Egyptian elements, were the guiding influence of the early Church.

CHAPTER V

THE BEGINNINGS OF CHRISTIANITY:
ARCHAEOLOGICAL EVIDENCE

In the last chapter some evidence was given of the rapid growth of Christianity, also of its peculiar character, and of the manner in which it was propagated by the earliest missionaries. So far however our evidence has been drawn from sources that are almost entirely Greek. It has already been pointed out that the old religion of Egypt was still fairly vigorous, and that away from Alexandria, even if many of the older gods had disappeared or become hellenized, the main doctrines about Osiris and Isis had been but slightly influenced by hellenism. In fact the old religion still possessed multitudes of devotees not only among the natives but also among those of mixed Graeco-Egyptian parentage and education. What of all the converts to Christianity from among these folk? Although the first appeal of the new religion seems to have been directed to those of entirely Hellenic and Alexandrine birth and education, there can be little doubt that all who were able to speak or read a little Greek would quickly make acquaintance with the new faith and would in turn hand their knowledge on, distorted and imperfect perhaps, to the *fellahîn* and uneducated natives. It is from these classes that our archaeological evidences are drawn, and although at present they are singularly scanty, they are nevertheless of the very greatest interest. Before discussing them however it may be well to point out in what manner the worshipper of the gods of Egypt would be likely to receive Christianity, as compared with followers of Roman or Hellenic cults.

The Egyptians differed from other nations of antiquity in that they believed in a continuation of life after death, concerning which they had very clear and definite ideas. To call this a belief in the "resurrection" is somewhat misleading. They thought that by carrying out certain definite rites they would be able to secure an unending existence for themselves in the underworld. By mummifying the body and preserving it from decomposition it was thought possible to preserve the ghostly entity of the individual for ever, and in order that the latter might not fail for want of nourishment, food-offerings were placed in the tomb and made available for the spirit by the magical ceremony called "The opening of the mouth." So that, if not of a very spiritual nature, their ideas as to a future life were well defined. This is also true of the "underworld" in which the spirits of the dead lived and moved[1]. Moreover the basis of all these ideas was the belief that Osiris, a god of human form, had himself once been slain and had by similar methods been able to overcome death. In short he "lived for ever" and ruled in the underworld as king of the dead. These main ideas had (as we have seen in the foregoing

---

[1] Although as we have seen there was some confusion between the Osirian and Heliopolitan systems.

chapters) survived the general religious decay of the
first two and a half centuries of our era, and instead of
the philosophic scepticism of the Greek, or the gloomy
visions of " Sheol " and the " pit " of orthodox Judaism,
the Egyptian still believed in an everlasting life after
death, in a resurrection of a spiritual body from a
mortal body. The Christian doctrine of the resurrection
therefore would come as nothing new to Egypt, and the
belief that the dead in Christ shall live in Christ would
be strangely familiar to all who were reared in the
Osirian creed. That the Egyptian religion was the
least spiritual in the world and relied mainly on what
is nothing more than the working of magic, does not
invalidate the outward resemblance between the two,
and it is only natural to suppose that when the new
faith began to replace the old, much of the outward
character and symbolism should still be retained,
in fact that where the old religion adequately represented an idea which seemed to be parallel with
something put forward by the new religion, the old
form of belief should be retained. That this admitted
semi-paganism into Christianity is undoubted, but from
what little we know of the early and disorganized
condition of Christianity in Egypt it would seem to
have been inevitable. Not only the continuation of
the practice of mummification by the early Christians
but the whole trend of archaeological discoveries goes
to support this contention. These last are still
unfortunately few and scattered. It will be our duty
in this chapter to survey and discuss all those that
have an important bearing on this subject, for it is
only by the collection of data such as these that we

are able to form some idea of the habits and customs
of the time when nearly all literary evidence fails us.
Our chief difficulty lies in the fact that many of these
objects lie so close to the border line of paganism that it
is difficult to state definitely to which source they
may be assigned. It will therefore be only fair to
give not only those that are certainly of Christian
origin but also those about which there is some
doubt.

As might be expected, the mummification of the
dead was a custom that was only given up by the
Christians gradually and with reluctance, and probably
did not come to an end until after the Arab conquest.
Christian mummies have been found in a large number
of places so widely scattered as Antinoë, Deir el-bahari,
Akhmim and the Oasis of Kharga, while it is evident
that the early Fathers at least did not look upon the
custom as altogether godless[1]. In fact there is every
reason to believe that the funerary customs of the early
Christians differed very little from those of their pagan
contemporaries. We have already seen how it was
the pagan custom to ferry the dead down the river to
the large necropoles such as Panopolis and Bompaë,
and how wooden tickets for identification were tied to
the mummies, sometimes written in Greek, sometimes
in Greek and Demotic, the latter usually containing in
addition a prayer that the deceased might live for ever
with Osiris Socharis. A wooden tablet of precisely the
same type as these is now in the Royal Museum at
Berlin, and bears the inscription " Psentheus, son of

---

[1] See Augustine: Sermo 361, *De Resurrectione Mortuorum.*

Apollonius, son of Patsēs" followed by the monogram ☧[1]. This is undoubtedly Christian, but unfortunately is undated. Thanks however to the other (pagan) tickets of the same style we are able to fix its age with a certain amount of accuracy. Dr Carl Schmidt considers that it must belong to the post-Constantinian age and bases his opinion on the fact that the monogram of Christ ☧ was not in general use until that period, being confined, at least so far as hitherto known inscriptions go, to the years 323–493. It is true that the monogram began to enjoy a sort of official usage at this date, but it is quite conceivable that it was employed before. If M. Gayet is right as to the dating of one of the bodies found at Antinoë[2], we have an example of the symbol employed as a seal during the third century. There is no reason why it should not have been in use sporadically before the beginning of the fourth century, and even if this were not the case it cannot be maintained that because a well-known Christian monogram has hitherto not appeared in inscriptions before a certain period it is impossible that it should appear before that time. We have however a more certain means of dating this ticket. Both the names it contains and the general palaeography resemble the texts on the tickets published by Spiegelberg[3] and by Hall[4]. Most of those described by the former date from the reign of Trajan and one of the

---

[1] C. Schmidt, "Ein altchristliches Mumienetikett," *Ä.Z.* xxxii. pp. 52 ff.

[2] *Annales du Musée Guimet*, xxx. 2, Pl. IV.

[3] *Ägyptische und Griechische Eigennamen aus Mumienetiketten der römischen Kaiserzeit*, Leipzig, 1901.

[4] *Greek Mummy Labels in the British Museum. P.S.B.A.* 1905.

latest is dated in "year 1" of Macrianus and Quietus, *i.e.* A.D. 260. Those of the second collection practically all belong to the third century[1]. The resemblance between these, which are nearly all from Akhmim (Panopolis) or Sûhâg (Bompaë), and the Christian ticket in question makes it impossible to doubt that the latter came from the same locality and is of approximately the same date; that is to say, some time in the third century if not earlier. It can certainly be no later. It is therefore clear from the evidence of this ticket that there were Christians in the neighbourhood of Akhmim during the third century whose mummied corpses were despatched by their relatives to the neighbouring cemeteries to lie in their last resting place beside their fellow townsmen and villagers who worshipped Osiris-Socharis. Several other tickets have been found which may be Christian but are not conclusively so. One such[2] is inscribed "Taêsai lived 28 years. She has gone to the shining (land)." This "shining land" has been thought to be the Christian heaven corresponding to the later φωτινὸς τόπος of Greek gravestones[3], but as has been pointed out by Hall[4] it may equally well refer to the place of the "illuminated ones," the *ikhu* of the old religion. Another ticket which is much more likely to be Christian is that of one Satripis who died in Alexandria[5]. The legend runs Σατρῖπις Ψενμαγῶτος

[1] A few belong to the late second century. Krebs (*Ä.Z.* xxxii. No. 18) points out one bearing an Indiction date, which must therefore belong to the fourth century.

[2] Berlin, No. 11820.   [3] Schmidt, *Ä.Z.* xxxii. p. 61.

[4] *Loc. cit.* p. 19.

[5] Berlin, No. 11827. See Schmidt, *loc. cit.*

ἐν ᾿Αλεξανδρείᾳ ἀναπαυσάμενος, the last word of which
was a very common Christian euphemism for dying, and
for this reason the ticket may safely be assigned to
a Christian origin. One or two others have been
published the Christian origin of which is extremely
doubtful, nevertheless there is good reason to hope
that more definite examples will turn up in time, more
especially as mummification was so generally practised
among the early Christians.

We have also seen in a former chapter how it was
the custom during the second and third centuries for
the rich to place the mummied body in a coffin with a
removable side, a fact which implies that the dead
were often kept for a considerable period in the house
and were exposed to the view of relatives and friends
from time to time[1]. Did the Christians also do this?
There seems to be some evidence in the affirmative.
Athanasius, speaking of the dislike entertained by
Anthony the great ascetic to mummification, says:—

"The Egyptians like to mummify and swathe in bandages
the bodies of the faithful who are dead, especially of the holy
martyrs; and not to hide them underground but to place them
on couches and keep them by them in the house, since they
think that in this way they honour the departed[2]."

This seems to point clearly to the fact that the early
Christians continued to conform to a general pagan
usage in vogue at the time, and one in which perhaps
originated the custom of preserving the remains of saints
in reliquaries, especially under the high altar, which in

[1] See H. R. Hall, in Hastings' *Encyclopaedia of Religion and
Ethics*, art. "Death and the disposal of the dead (Egyptian)."
[2] Athanasius, *Vita Ant.* (Migne, x. p. 967.)

modern Roman custom has much of the tomb about it
and is often made in the shape of a sarcophagus.
Nevertheless it was more usual to bury the dead at
once, generally in shallow brick-lined graves, or in
desert cliff-tombs, to some of which were attached
chapels. It is to these funerary customs that we owe
some of the most interesting of our archaeological
knowledge. It may be as well to go into what is already
known of the subject in some detail.

The two most important sites where cemeteries
containing Christian graves have been investigated
on a large scale are Antinoë and Akhmim[1]. The
former has yielded results of the utmost interest, for
which we are indebted to M. Gayet who excavated
it for the Musée Guimet in Paris during the years
1896—1900[2]. Unfortunately these valuable results
have not been placed at the disposal of students in
a very scientific and orderly manner, so that in some
ways we are more mystified than ever about the date
of the objects found owing to the excavator's want of
precision and his insufficient observation of the position
and "sequence" of the finds. Moreover confusion
becomes worse confounded when we recall his ideas
on the subject of Christianity in Egypt. In spite
of the fact that Christianity was well established in
Oxyrhynchus beyond all doubt early in the second
century (in a town moreover which is only about 60 miles
from Antinoë), in spite of the evidence afforded by the
mummy-tickets and by the *libelli* issued to those who
had recanted during the Decian persecution, in spite

---

[1] The ancient Panopolis.
[2] *Annales du Musée Guimet*, Tome xxx.

of the activity of Christian Gnostic teachers and the influence exercised by the catechetical school during the early part of the third century, M. Gayet says that tombs of a certain kind "se classent toutes dans le courant des IVe et IVe (*sic*) siècles, et s'échelonnent de 382 à 460. Cela nous reporte au second siècle du christianisme égyptien, *la conversion n'ayant commencé qu'avec la persécution de Dioclétien*—295 à 311—et l'édit consacrant la paix de l'Église[1]." This opinion, of course, somewhat accounts for M. Gayet's loose use of the much abused term "Byzantine," although even then it is difficult to comprehend such a sentence as this: "les autres franchement *byzantines* donnent les images complexes du répertoire symbolique des *premiers chrétiens*[2]." This confusion of terms only renders more difficult the already uncertain task of dating many of these objects.

The necropolis of Antinoë may roughly be divided into two portions, the first occupying the low-lying ground near the town itself, the second consisting of rock-cut tombs situated high up in the desert hills which form a circus behind the plain and run round to the N.W. into a steep cliff overhanging the Nile. A complete series of tombs appears to have been excavated, dating from the time of the foundation of the city by Hadrian up to about the end of the fifth century. Some of these are undoubtedly Christian. The graves, either brick chambers for the rich, or plain trenches for the poor, contained the bodies of persons of varying rank, both bandaged and covered

---

[1] *Loc. cit.* p. 38.   The italics are mine.
[2] *Loc. cit.* p. 27.   The italics are mine.

with shawls and scarves. The bodies of the earlier
Roman period however were simply wrapped in grave-
clothes, and either there was a plaster mask on the face
or the outer wrappings bore a painted portrait of the
deceased. Among these wrappings of the earlier period
is one of considerable interest. It bears a painted
portrait of a woman named Krispina with a handsome
oval face and the hair dressed somewhat after the
manner of the Antonine empresses. The left hand
raised to the level of the breast holds a symbol of life
('ankh ☥) which is certainly of a peculiar shape suggesting
an intermediate form between the ancient symbol and the
Christian cross. If the reader looks closely at M. Gayet's
illustration it will be noticed that the circular portion
forming the top is raised slightly and does not spring
immediately from the junction of the stem and the cross
pieces, thus forming an 'ankh of the shape typical on early
Christian designs. Down the sides of the covering on
the panels, where as a rule at this period various deities
of the dead are depicted, it is somewhat remarkable
that only floral designs are represented. It might
therefore be conjectured that this woman was a member
of one of the early Christian communities. Certainly
the form of the 'ankh is peculiar, and we know that this
symbol was dear to the Egyptian Christians; it was
never really ousted by the cross, but passed into later
iconography as the *crux ansata*. Nevertheless this
mummy-covering must perhaps remain one of the
doubtfully Christian objects, in spite of what we know
of the pagan forms that were adopted into early
Christian symbolism. The bad preservation of the
lower part and the illegibility of the inscription make

it still more impossible to find out anything more
definite about it, and although fragments of scenes in
the Pompeian style remain visible, which M. Gayet
thinks are connected with the cycle of representations
relative to the happiness of the elect, we have to
confess that it may possibly have belonged to a devout
member of the Greek cult of Osiris.   Another burial,
that of a woman whose name M. Gayet reads as
"Euphemiaan[1]," is supposed by him to be connected
with the declining years of the gnostic communities
of Basilides and Valentinus.   But M. Gayet's sole
evidence for this is apparently a peculiar ivory object
which he styles an "ivoire gnostique[2]."   Why this
object should be gnostic M. Gayet does not tell us, and
there certainly seems little or no reason for calling it
so.   What is much more important, and what seems
to have been overlooked, is the fact that at least two
of the seals which sealed the bandages of "Euphemiaan"
are stamped with the sacred monogram ☧ which, taken
in connexion with the legend "Be at peace," em-
broidered on the deceased's shoes, clearly points to
Christian influence, whether gnostic or otherwise.
M. Gayet's contention that this burial is not later
than the year 250 and is perhaps considerably earlier
may be correct[3], and the fact that some of the seals bear
the impression of a female figure holding an urn reversed
is quite in accordance with the mingling of pagan
and Christian symbolism characteristic of the period.

[1] Euphemiana?   [2] *Loc. cit.* p. 32.
[3] In view of the consideration adduced with regard to the use of
the Christian monogram on p. 103.

Two other graves from the lower ground at Antinoë
are also of peculiar interest. The first, that of a
woman, consisted of a narrow vaulted cell about
2 metres long and ·80 wide built of unbaked brick.
According to the excavator, remains of stucco on an
outside niche bore three lines of rudely traced inscription
as follows : ✠ Ἐκοιμήθη μακαρια Θαιας...Θεσσαλ....
On the western wall at the foot of the body was a
cross flanked by A and ധ. With the body was found
a large jar bearing the inscription MIKH, two reed
baskets, a peculiar object in ivory and wood, and a
wooden symbol of life (ʿankh) or crux ansata[1].

According to M. Gayet the other grave is identical
in appearance but without any inscriptions. In it was
the body of a man wearing a coarse brown robe and
black mantle, and sandals furnished with nails. Round
his waist, his ankles, and arms were iron bands; from
his neck hung a cross. A piece of pottery in the tomb
bore the inscription Σαραπιων Κορνωσθαλου[2]. There
can therefore be little doubt that this Sarapion was
one of the early anchorites or ascetics who chose this
method of binding himself in iron bands in order to
mortify the flesh.

It is however in the contents of the first of these
two graves that we shall find our chief interest. In
connexion with the presence of a basket and an
amphora in the tomb M. Gayet recalls a passage in
Saint Jerome, "Nihil illo ditius qui corpus Domini
portat in vimineo canistro et sanguinem in vitro," and
reminds us of the Acts of the Council of Hippo which
sat in 393 and amongst other things condemned the

[1] *Loc. cit.* p. 36.   [2] *ib.* p. 39.

practice prevalent among oriental Christians of placing
the holy elements in the coffins of the dead.   That
these objects contained bread and wine is probable.
Was this simply a re-adjustment of the old pagan
custom of burying food-offerings with the dead ?   It
is possible that as the material body was thought by
the old Egyptians to require sustenance in the underworld so the Egyptian Christians thought that the
souls of the dead required the spiritual food of the
Eucharist.   In connexion with this it may be recalled
that many of the outer tomb-chambers in the Christian
cemetery in the Oasis of el-Kharga contain a niche
for the reception of food-offerings similar to those in
pagan tombs[1].   It is however more likely that the
explanation of the presence of eucharistic vessels in
tombs lies in some of the mystic Gnostic sacraments.
In the Gnostic gospel known as *Pistis Sophia*, the
Saviour speaks of a great mystery greater than all
other mysteries.   In another Gnostic work of the same
kind this mystery appears as the so-called " Sacrament
of the Ineffable One," in which Christ takes bread and
wine and pronounces a long series of mystic words.
If a man know this mystery (which is nothing more
or less than a magical spell), or if the friends of the
dead man are able to perform the sacrament for him,
it will procure remission of all sins, even the most
heinous.   As bread and wine play an important part
in the sacrament, it is a legitimate conjecture that
this woman was buried with an outfit for the
celebration of this or some closely related Gnostic

[1] C. S. Myers, in *Man*, 1901, No. 91 (p. 113).

mystery[1]. This grave is moreover of somewhat late
date and is probably to be assigned to the end of the
fourth century, when Gnosticism had not only reached
its fullest and most fantastic development but was
fast on the wane and only likely to be found still
flourishing in provincial centres.

The peculiar wooden and ivory object found with
this burial[2] is also of interest. It is arranged in three
tiers, two of which contain holes at regular intervals
into which a peg was perhaps inserted. It is surmounted by a small cross. M. Gayet thinks this is
a kind of primitive rosary, a "compte prières."
Presumably by moving the peg from hole to hole
it was possible to check the prayers or verses of
scripture being recited. It was certainly a more
convenient method than that said to have been
adopted by the early ascetics of filling their mouths
with pebbles and spitting one out as each verse of a
psalm was recited.

One more curious thing with regard to this burial
is the fact that the hands of the deceased grasped a
small cruciform flower classified by M. Bonnet as
Anastatica hierochuntina[3], a common desert plant
which lies ordinarily dead and lifeless, but on contact
with the slightest moisture blossoms at once into life.
M. Gayet thinks this is symbolic of the resurrection
and is the origin of the mystic rose of Jericho which
in Crusading times was thought to bloom once a year
on the eve of the Nativity of our Lord. The first of
these suppositions is probably correct, although the

---

[1] Gayet, *l.c.* pl. xviii. 1.   [2] See later p. 117.
[3] *Annales du Musée Guimet*, xxx. 1, p. 155.

latter is extremely doubtful. As a matter of fact bodies of the Graeco-Roman period were frequently represented either in painting or in plaster relief as clasping a wreath of flowers in one hand, and this may very likely be a continuation of the custom, only with this special flower chosen in order to represent symbolically the resurrection.

With regard to the name of this burial and that of the similar one hard by it is exceedingly disappointing that it has apparently been impossible to publish a photograph of the plaster containing the name *Thaias*. Not only would it have helped to remove doubt as to whether this burial was in any way connected with the famous courtesan Thaïs of Alexandria and the monk Serapion who led her from her life of easy virtue[1], but we should also have possessed palaeographical evidence of the greatest importance which might have helped not only to date this burial itself but possibly also to decide the question whether it was contemporaneous with the other. The large fragment bearing the name "Sarapion son of Kornosthalos" may not refer to the body with which it was found at all : at least it seems curious that the only memorial left of the deceased should be on a potsherd. His name may also have been on the stucco or elsewhere and have been lost, but the fact that a name on an ostrakon was found with the body is not absolute evidence that this name referred to the burial in which it was found. Moreover Sarapion or Serapion is an extremely common name of the period. As it is, therefore, considerable scepticism may be felt as to

[1] For the authorities on Thaïs and Serapion, see Nau, *Annales du Musée Guimet*, xxx. 1, p. 51 ff.

the claim of the Musée Guimet that these two bodies are the actual remains of this famous pair whose history passed down from ascetic records to the tales of the troubadours and story-tellers of the Middle Ages; and it must be admitted that this scepticism is justified. Why has one burial an outfit either for food-offerings or some sacramental ceremony, and the other none? Even if the second burial had been plundered, it is hardly likely that an orthodox Christian (and there is every reason to believe that the hero of the Thaïs tale was orthodox) would at the end of the fourth century be buried with such funeral furniture or would sanction it in the grave of one whom he had converted. Again, while Sarapion was clearly an ascetic, the body of Thaias seems to have received much more luxurious burial than that which would have been given to a strict solitary, as, according to the tale, the repentant courtesan became. It is true, M. Gayet says: "Je n'ai aucun document me permettant d'identifier Thaïs [*sic*!] d'Antinoë à la Thaïs historique": but he adds "je n'en ai aucun, non plus, m'autorisant à nier la possibilité de cette identification[1]." The authorities of the Musée Guimet have, however, maintained this identification, which is based on a groundwork of facts of very little scientific value.

The later excavations of tombs in the cliffs were in some ways not so successful as those on the lower ground owing to the soil having fallen away in many places. Nevertheless a remarkable series of tombs was found. Some of these tombs had brick chapels before them, eight of which were Christian, according to

[1] *Loc. cit.* p. 38.

M. Gayet. The interiors of these latter were apparently covered with frescoes which the excavator says

"belong to the category of the primitive symbolism of the Catacombs. These are the Good Shepherd, the praying woman, the dove, the peacock, the trees of the garden of paradise and figures of the saints. Lastly the cross either plain, or bearing the nimbus of a crown, or garlanded with flowers[1]."

Curiously enough however these frescoes seem to have been painted over with a layer of plaster and were thus rendered invisible to those who entered the tomb. M. Gayet suggests two alternative reasons for this strange procedure on the part of the Christian decorators. Either the idea was to hide the frescoes from pagans and so avoid desecration and persecution, or the scenes were nothing but a continuation of the magical pictures on the walls of the pharaonic tombs altered to fit in with Christian ideas: their magical effect being equally efficient whether they were covered up or not. The former view, which presupposes that the chapels are anterior to the reign of Constantine, is much the more probable, although the fragmentary condition of the frescoes seems to have prevented any just estimate of their date. M. Gayet at any rate seems to think that they are primitive.

A great number of bodies of the Graeco-Roman period were found in the rock caves, although none of them appear to have belonged to Christians. M. Gayet divides these burials into two types. In the earlier the bodies were dipped into a bath of bitumen and certain parts were afterwards covered with gold leaf. The bodies were then bandaged and re-bandaged in

[1] I translate M. Gayet's description; *loc. cit.* p. 121.

spiral or interlaced patterns and a fresh coat of bitumen
applied. Over this came a fresh layer of bandages,
and finally the body was covered with a fine cloth
painted with scenes in various colours and gilding, or
a plaster mask simulating the features of the deceased
was placed over the head and shoulders. In the
later type the bodies are not dipped in bitumen and
not enveloped in bandages but simply clothed, presumably in tunics and shawls. Now the first class of these
is well known and has been described in Mr Edgar's
catalogue of the Cairo collection[1]. To it must be
assigned the cloth with the beautiful portrait of
Krispina carrying the *crux ansata* already described
(p. 108) and also the curious figure of the so-called
Christian priest found at Deir el-bahari which will be
discussed later (p. 126 ff.). To the latter class apparently
belong the burials of Thaias and Sarapion. Now the
former type, we know, did not survive much longer
than the first quarter of the third century[2], so that we
are thus able to guess at approximate dates for some
of these interments, or at least to say that burials with
painted wrappings over bandages or with plaster-
modelled faces are not later than 250 A.D., whereas the
burials in scarves and shawls without the use of
bitumen date from about that time and onward[3].

---

[1] Edgar, *Catalogue général des Antiquités du Musée du Caire:
Graeco-Egyptian Coffins.*

[2] See Mr Edgar's preface, p. x., *loc. cit.*

[3] It is interesting to note in passing that at least one painted
board of the Hawara type already referred to occurred at Antinoë
which cannot be much later than the age of Hadrian and therefore not far removed from the date of the foundation of the
town. M. Gayet by the way (*l. c.* p. 132 f.) calls the man for whom

Other burials at Antinoë are of considerable interest. That called by M. Gayet "Sépulture d'une femme byzantine[1]" was found in a cavern half in the mountain and half in the plain with a ruined chapel ornamented with frescoes of the praying woman, the trees of the garden of paradise, the dove and the peacock etc. Several fragments were found which " se rattachent au symbolisme des premiers siècles de l'Église d'Alexandrie." If this is the case how does M. Gayet reconcile the fact that he calls the owner "une dame byzantine"? The most interesting object found in this tomb is a tablet similar to the "compte prières" of Thaias, executed in cedar wood and inlaid with bone and mother-of-pearl. One face is rounded, the other is flat and bears on the surface a niche in raised ivory plaques surmounted by a gable inclosing a cross of mother-of-pearl; below is an ivory arrangement similar to that of Thaias for marking the number of prayers recited. Again, another burial called by M. Gayet "Sépulture d'un chevalier byzantin[2]," contained the body of a man wearing a tunic and leggings with high boots and girt about with scarves, "un spécimen complet du costume porté par les chevaliers byzantins au Ve siècle de notre ère." Yet the decoration of a vase found in this tomb also belongs "au répertoire des premiers temps du symbolisme d'Église d'Alexandrie," that is to say to the second century! These two

---

this painting was made " Aπoλλων ευψυχι " (sic !): the second word is a very well-known one in funerary inscriptions of this period and was addressed to the deceased by way of farewell, having nothing whatever to do with his name. This man was called Apollôn simply.

[1] L. c. p. 129.   [2] ib. p. 130.

statements are irreconcileable, and it must be presumed
that M. Gayet intends the first to be accepted, although
the present writer would tentatively suggest the later
part of the fourth century, in view of the peculiar square
appearance of the carving on a piece of wood found in
the tomb, a style which differs considerably from the
later rounded and often careless work.

The chapel was painted with frescoes of praying
figures and crosses garlanded with flowers. The rock
corridor was decorated with vine tendrils painted in
black, which M. Gayet thinks recalls the vines sometimes
painted in pharaonic tombs and nearly always coloured
black also. At the entrance were some great jars one of
which, already referred to as said to bear the symbolism
of the early church of Alexandria, has painted on it a fish
swimming among the papyrus beds. Perhaps the most
interesting object of all however is a little terra-cotta
model of several figures reclining at a table spread with
a banquet. M. Gayet thinks this is a model of the *agape*[1].
Taken in connexion with the large jars found at the
door of the tomb, we have here evidence either of some
rite for nourishing the souls of the dead with spiritual
food such as was found in the tomb of Thaias, or of
some sacramental ceremony on behalf of the dead. In
connexion with this it is interesting to note a very
curious statement in the will of one Aurelius Colluthus,
a Christian who lived during the first half of the fifth
century and was buried at Antinoë. The will written
on papyrus was found in his tomb. After stating that
he has drawn up the document in the Greek language,

[1] The *agape* had in the fifth century disappeared, the Eucharistic
feast having taken its place entirely.

being in sound health mentally and bodily, in the
presence of seven witnesses, he proceeds to appoint
his wife Tisoia his sole heiress to all his property real
and personal. He then says, "I desire that my body
shall be wrapped in a cere-cloth and that *celebration be
made of the holy offerings and funerary repasts for
the repose of my soul before Almighty God*." This is
exceedingly interesting as a very early example of a
eucharistic ceremony for the repose of the dead. It
would however be going too far to suggest that
"repose" was equivalent to the "nourishment" of the
spiritual body by spiritual food, although discoveries
at Antinoë point to some such idea being prevalent.

A number of other semi-pagan objects were found
in the Christian cemetery of Antinoë, such as seals im-
pressed with various symbols, gnostic figures, scorpions,
whips, figures of pagan gods, the cross, and imperial
portraits. One fragment is perhaps of particular
interest, a piece of wood bearing the letters XM̅Γ.
This according to M. Gayet represents the words
Χριστὸν Μαρία γεννᾷ, *i.e.* "Mary begets Christ."
As a matter of fact a great number of interpretations
have been given of this curious monogram[1]. As the
form XC̅ . MAPIA . ΓENNA also occurs, M. Gayet's
rendering, although more grammatical, is discounted.
In this form it appears to be a kind of theosophical
expression for the triad "Father, Mother, Son," but
this interpretation is also in any case extremely
doubtful[2]. Another suggestion is that it represents

[1] See Smirnoff in *Berliner Philologische Wochenschrift*, Aug. 1906,
No. 33/4, also Nestle's article in the same journal.

[2] Wessely understands it as Χριστοῦ Μαρία γέννα, "Mary Mother of
Christ" (*Mitth. aus der Samml. Pap. Rainer*, VI. 118).

the words, Christ, Michael, and Gabriel, but although
X frequently stands for the word Χριστος no example
is known of the names of the archangels being ab-
breviated in a similar manner. It is more probable
that those who seek the interpretation in resolving the
monogram (when not written out) into an acrostic of
numerals are nearest the solution. Such acrostics were
frequently employed not only by Gnostic Christians but
also by mystic religious societies among the pagans.
ΧΜΓ represents the number 643, which in its turn may
be resolved into either of three interpretations (1) Ἅγιος
ὁ Θεός, (2) Νέος Ἥλιος, a reference perhaps to Constantine, or (3) Θεὸς βοηθός, a common funerary device of the
time. We know that the later Copts misunderstood it
and explained ΧΜΓ and the variant ΧΜΓΘ (643 + 9)
as ἡ ἁγία τριὰς θ[εός]. A quite different suggestion
has been made by M. J. J. Smirnoff, who thinks that
ΧΜΓ is a distortion of the Hebrew word אחד,
meaning " one," which was employed frequently by the
Jewish mystics to veil the divine name. Certainly
the resemblance between א and X and ד and Γ is very
striking, but that between M and ח is not so apparent,
although the inscription quoted by Smirnoff ΕΙΣ ΘΕΟΣ
ΧΜΓ ΜΟΝΟΣ tells greatly in favour of this argument[1].
It is in any case interesting to find this mystic symbolism in use at Antinoë.

[1] On the whole, however, the explanation ΧΜΓ = 643 = ἅγιος ὁ
Θεός is perhaps the most probable. Cf. Smirnoff, in *Trans.*
(Soöbstchenie) *Russ. Palest. Soc.* xiii. 2, 1, quoted by H. R. Hall,
*Greek and Coptic Inscriptions of the Christian Period in the British
Museum*, p. 2. Εἰς Θεὸς ΧΜΓ μόνος then = εἰς Θεός, ἅγιος ὁ Θεός, μόνος
(ὁ Θεός). It was then also understood and sometimes spelt out as
χ(ριστο)ς Μ(αρια) γ(εννα).

Taken altogether, therefore, the excavations at
Antinoë must rank among the most important discoveries of early Christian customs and beliefs. We
are at least able to gain a glimpse of the actual burial
usages of both the pagan and Christian communities
from the third to the fifth centuries. But Antinoë
must have been, as its foundation would imply, a centre
chiefly of Graeco-Roman life or at any rate of Egyptian
life with a strong veneer of hellenism, and this doubtless accounts for the extraordinary jumble of Hellenic and
Egyptian elements in both pagan and Christian burials.

Let us now turn to the objects which the cemetery
of Akhmim has yielded. Unfortunately in this case
we are practically without the aid that only scientific
excavation can give, for the site has been plundered
by native spoilers and the finds have made their
way into European Museums through the hands of
dealers. M. Maspero from time to time conducted
excavations on the site and has briefly published the
results[1], but we have to rely for the most part on those
objects from the various collections which have been
published in catalogues. The chief of these are Forrer's
Die frühchristlichen Alterthümer von Achmim-Panopolis
and *Die Gräber- und Textilfunde von Achmim-Panopolis*,
both of which contain a large number of objects from
the Christian cemetery of Akhmim, but here again we
are confronted with the difficulty of dating many of
these antiquities with anything like certainty.

The cemetery itself was undoubtedly inaugurated
early in the first century of our era, when the neighbouring Ptolemaic burial ground was abandoned, and

[1] In the *Bulletin de l'Institut égyptien.*

continued in use until the eighth or ninth century. The bodies, of nearly all dates covered by this period, were buried, dressed in their richest and best clothing, in graves about one and a half metres beneath the soil. The majority were simply laid in the trench without coffins and without wood or stone coverings, but in the case of some of the richer burials the corpse was protected by a slab of stone. The method of preservation was not by bitumen but apparently by soaking in natron, nevertheless it is rather to the fine dry sand of Egypt than to any of the embalming processes that we owe the fine condition of bodies and clothes alike. It is due to this cause also that we possess the magnificent series of textiles from this site which are a revelation of the skill and artistic knowledge for which the Panopolites were famous. There is no doubt that Forrer's contention that the earliest of these date back to the times of the first Roman emperors is correct. They are to be distinguished from the later tapestries by the inwoven designs, always inspired by *classical* motives and often formal copies of classical mosaics. These designs too are almost invariably carried out in one colour, a dark purplish blue, and represent, either in medallions or borders, animals, men, and mythical creatures, marine deities also being special favourites. Of the earlier stuffs of this first period, that is to say of the first and second centuries, it is difficult to say whether any bear definite Christian designs, but this is of course no proof that none of these belonged to Christians. Apart from the evidence of the existence of a Christian community during the second and third centuries afforded by the mummy-

tickets already mentioned, there occur as designs on
these stuffs such subjects as the cross, the fish, the dove,
and the hare, and the three latter, it is noteworthy,
were peculiarly employed in early Christian design as
furtive symbols of the faith. Accordingly where they
occur here it may be argued that they might be from
an early Christian burial. It will never however be
possible to come to any definite conclusion about these,
because the earliest Christians freely employed pagan
designs and were at the same time very restrained in
their use of Christian symbolism, but one little design
of frequent occurrence, namely that of two doves on
either side of a cup, the latter perhaps having a
eucharistic meaning, seems to be more definitely of
Christian origin. This is the more probable when we
consider how this type persisted in Christian tapestry
down to a much later period, and also when we find in
the fifth and sixth centuries doves, hares and fishes
still employed but the pagan deities and figures
changed into military saints and representations of
the Saviour.

Perhaps one of the most noteworthy designs on cloth
is one which must belong, judging both by its form and
by the name inscribed on it, either to the third or at the
latest to the first part of the fourth century. This design
consists of a large *crux ansata* flanked by two small
crosses; in the centre of the larger cross are woven
the words ⲦⲀⲘⲒⲚ ⲚⲈⲰⲦⲈⲢⲀ, *i.e.* "Tamin the younger [1]."

[1] Forrer, *l. c.* xiv. 1 and 2. The name Tamin is old Egyptian,
meaning "She who belongs to (the God) Min," who was identified by
the Greeks with Pan. Such a name, though pagan, would be quite
ordinarily borne by a Christian. The corresponding masculine form,
Pamin, was the name of a well-known Coptic abbot.

A very similar design is shown in another fragment, which has, however, a rude ☥ in the centre of the *crux ansata*. These again are a striking witness to the persistence with which the Egyptian Christians clung to the use of their ancient Egyptian hieroglyphic of life as a form of the Christian cross, and the fact that it is repeatedly found as one of the principal forms of decoration in Egyptian Christian art for several centuries after this date proves how deep-rooted its popularity continued to be. The symbol ☥ occurs also on a terra-cotta lamp from this site which by its general form and shape cannot be of much later date than the beginning of the third century[1]. Forrer however thinks[2] that the Christian monogram is a later addition of the Constantinian age scratched on to the lamp after firing, which accordingly brings it, as far as the Christian symbolism goes, down to the fourth century, during and after which period hundreds of lamps were made in Akhmim bearing the ☥ stamped on them as decoration.

But more primitive symbols occur at Akhmim. A ring of early shape (probably of the second century) has incised on the bezel an anchor and two fishes, while a model anchor comes from a neighbouring tomb. There are also wooden combs with a carved representation of Thecla between two lions. Not the least interesting object from this site is a small figure, described by Forrer[3] as made of tin, bandaged like a mummy with the hands folded on the breast. Forrer

[1] *C. I. L.* Vol. xv. p. 783.

[2] *Die frühchristlichen Alterthümer von Achmim*, p. 11.

[3] *Loc. cit.* p. 16, Taf. xiii, No. 19; [in the description of the plates on p. 7 it is described as of lead].

thinks this is intended for a figure of Lazarus placed
in the grave (in the same manner as figures of Osiris
were among the pagans) as a type of the resurrection.
This figure can certainly have no connexion with the
ushabti figures of pharaonic times, which were placed
in the grave in lieu of the servants and slaves originally
slaughtered in order to accompany a great man to the
underworld when he died[1], for the use of these figures
was discontinued before Ptolemaic times and would
have lapsed into oblivion by this period. If the figure
is from a Christian grave it is much more likely to be
connected with some form or figure of our Saviour as
dead, in the same way as Osiris was represented as
dead, such a figure naturally being considered a very
potent amulet against the forces of corruption. It is
however equally likely that this figure is not Christian
at all but connected with the pagan cult of Osiris.
It is not by any means impossible that the early
Christians of Akhmim buried amulets as types of the
resurrection similar to those of their pagan brothers;
indeed there seems to be some evidence for thinking
that they were not above placing in their graves figures
of Osiris himself, for one such figure at least seems to
have been found in a Christian grave[2]. Unfortunately
the *provenance* of this little tin mummy-figurine is so
uncertain that it is idle to speculate on its use, and
it only affords another example of the importance of
precise and scientific excavation.

---

[1] See L. W. King and H. R. Hall, *Egypt and Western Asia in
the Light of Recent Discoveries* (S.P.C.K. 1907), pp. 68, 329.

[2] *Die frühchristlichen Alterthümer*, p. 16.

It is possible even that we have a still more extraordinary example of religious syncretism than the foregoing. During the course of the excavation of the great temple at Deir el-bahari (which was partly built over in Christian times by a Coptic monastery) M. Naville brought to the light of day a very remarkable mummy[1]. The exterior is decorated by the head of a man in painted plaster wearing a wreath, and the body is covered by a piece of woven material painted in various colours on a white ground. On this the hands of the deceased are represented, the right holding a cup containing a red liquid, the left holding what has generally been taken for a handful of corn-ears. Hung from the neck is a peculiar object the significance of which is uncertain. On the left shoulder is the 卍 or *swastika* emblem, while the lower part of the robe is occupied by a scene representing two jackal-headed gods, probably Anubis and Upuaut, adoring the sacred bark of Socharis. M. Naville states [2] that this mummy was found with others which are undoubtedly Christian and the date of which is proved by the presence of Greek and Coptic mummy tickets. He further states that a *Coptic* label was attached to this particular mummy, and considers that the cup of wine and the ears of corn are emblems of the eucharist. Now a very similar mummy in the Cairo museum has recently been published in the Catalogue of Graeco-Egyptian mummies and coffins by Mr Edgar[3]. Here we have

[1] Now in the Musée Guimet in Paris.

[2] *Deir el-bahari*, II. p. 5. See also *Archaeological Report of the Egypt Exploration Fund*, 1893–94, p. 4.

[3] *Catalogue du Musée du Caire: Graeco-Egyptian Coffins, Masks, Portraits*, Plate XLVI.

a similar style of plaster head and the hands represented
as holding the cup and apparently a wreath of corn-
ears.   Below is the same scene of the jackal-headed
gods worshipping the boat of Socharis, and the *swastika*
appears on the left shoulder.   It differs from the Deir
el-bahari mummy in that the emblem of the solar
wings hangs from the neck and a small dark brown
amphora is represented on the right breast.

Now these two mummies are of considerable
importance.   In the first place if they are those of
Christians they represent a more extraordinary jumbling
of Christianity and paganism than even the most
fantastic of the Gnostic sects betray[1].   If on the other
hand they are pagan the emblems held in the hands
differentiate them from all similar mummies of the
same kind, nor do these emblems seem explicable from
any known rite or custom of the multitude of pagan
cults and religious societies that existed at that time.
Let us in the first place consider the date of these
objects.   M. Naville himself does not seem to have
realized the importance of the Deir el-bahari mummy
from the point of view of the history of paganism and
Christianity, and it is extremely regrettable that the
ticket attached to it has never been published[2].   This

[1] Although it must be remembered that the bark of the moon is
described in detail in the Gnostic gospel of *Pistis Sophia*, leaving no
doubt as to its purely Egyptian symbolism.

[2] Mr Crum has kindly supplied the reading of a tessera presumably
attached to this mummy—

Παχωνς Τεσαρ
μεσησε΄ Επωνυχος
απο κωμε Τερνουθε

This is a Greek ticket, probably of the third century.

might have afforded a good and definite clue to the date. M. Naville states that a *Coptic* label was attached but that Greek labels were also found from the same burying place. Now it is almost inconceivable that this mummy should be as late as the Coptic period and quite impossible for it to belong to the age of the Coptic *deir* or monastery that was built over the great temple of Hatshepsut. Nor is it likely, quite apart from considerations of the style and technique of the painting and plaster work, that adoration of the bark of Socharis would ever have appeared on the shroud of a Coptic monk. The twilight of the ancient gods had become impenetrable night by that period. It is obvious therefore that an earlier date must be sought if we are to have any satisfactory explanation of these peculiarities, and without going into details a date of between 250 and 300 may be safely assumed. Mr Edgar in discussing the relationship of the Cairo with the Deir el-bahari mummy[1], both of which he considers very likely to have come from the same site, seems, as far as dating goes, to have been misled by M. Naville's "Coptic" label. He considers that, so far as our knowledge goes, these plaster heads and busts do not date, as a series, later than the second quarter of the third century, but that these two particular mummies and one or two plaster busts of a similar style belong to a "Byzantine" type of the fourth or even fifth century. This implies a gap in the series of a century and a half or more. It seems far more natural to suppose that this so-called Byzantine style is but a decadent and elaborated form of the foregoing types, and belongs to

[1] *Loc. cit.* p. xi.

the latter half of the third century, following on them in natural sequence. It is quite true, as Mr Edgar suggests, that the wreaths and ear-rings seem more akin to the forms of early Byzantine portraiture, but this evidence is strongly counterbalanced by the execution of the painting on the shrouds, especially of the jackal-god scene, which is almost identical with pagan work of the same kind of the third century. Considered in this light the two mummies appear as the last stage of plaster work of head and bust for funerary purposes, and are probably to be assigned to a date between 250 and 300 A.D.

But when we turn to the mythological or religious import of these objects we are involved in even greater uncertainty. M. Naville thought that the wine cup and wheat ears were emblems of the eucharist, and this has been endorsed by M. Guimet, who even goes further and says that the white robe is sacerdotal and the *swastika* is emblematic of eastern influence. This, as Mr Edgar says[1], is going altogether too far. Mr Edgar himself is inclined to believe in the Christian hypothesis. But it is difficult to reconcile such syncretism in the fifth or even the fourth century, the dates which he offers for these designs. It seems almost incredible that a Christian should be represented as grasping the emblems of the eucharist and at the same time be decorated with the cult scenes of Socharis, unless he belonged to some of the early fantastic Gnostic sects who might conceivably have employed this mixed symbolism. It must also be remembered that the *swastika* was used as a Christian emblem from the

---

[1] *Graeco-Egyptian Coffins* (*Cairo Cat.*, 1905), p. x. f.

earliest times, and not only in the Roman catacombs, for it has also been found on tapestry at Akhmim and as a frequent funerary ornament in Phrygia[1] and Pontus in quite early times. The fact also that one and probably both mummies came from a site used for Christian burials is a considerable argument in favour of a Christian or semi-Christian origin. Nor is this inherently improbable when we consider the tendency to semi-paganism evidenced by the early Egyptian Christians and the activity of the Gnostic teachers. On the other hand there can be very little doubt that the object held in the left hand of the Cairo mummy is nothing more than a funerary wreath tied with ribbon, and the cup of wine has its parallel in the cups and grapes represented in the pagan funeral repasts of an earlier period. This is well illustrated by a comparison with No. 3321 b of Mr Edgar's catalogue. It is however almost impossible to come to any definite conclusion in the matter, and until some similar designs with more direct mythological or religious symbolism are found, these two figures must remain quite uncertain.

It may be admitted that the archaeological finds from early Christian cemeteries in Egypt may fairly be said to be bewildering and afford very insufficient data for theorizing. Everything however seems to point to the fact that, as far as funerary customs are concerned, the syncretism of the age is evident not only in early Christian art, but also in early Christian beliefs. We

[1] See Miss Margaret Ramsay, *Isaurian and East Phrygian Art*, Figs. 12 ff. (in Sir William Ramsay's *Studies in the Eastern Roman Provinces*, p. 34 ff.).

must also bear in mind, when considering these objects, the notorious activity of the Gnostic teachers during the second and third centuries, and the conservative character of the Egyptians themselves.   In the first case there existed an active propaganda of various systems which, however grotesque some of them may have become, had as their object the spreading of religious syncretism and the teaching of esoteric mysteries which were to explain not only the mysteries of the Christian faith but those of the pagan religions as well.   In Gnosticism all religions found a place, hence it is perfectly conceivable that a man might be buried, for instance, with the symbolism of the boat of Socharis and eucharistic emblems depicted on his shroud.   In the second case, the conservative and non-philosophical character of the Egyptians themselves might easily lead to the perpetuation of the old native beliefs, especially with regard to funerary customs and the deeply rooted ideas concerning a future life, under a thin disguise of Christianity.   That these things would be impossible to an educated Greek who had become a convert is obvious, but the natives, who for all we know may have from the first been largely under the influence of semi-gnostic or at least ignorant and irregular missionaries, would easily become converts to a religion which based its faith, as did their own, on a Deity who had risen from the dead and in whom all might hope to gain immortality.   The essential difference between the two religions, that the resurrection of the one was a *spiritual* resurrection and that of the other *magical*, occurred probably neither to missionary nor convert; with the result that the

9—2

native Christian continued his magical practices of mummifying the dead and equipping them with food-offerings still in the belief that these ceremonies were as essential in the new faith as in the old.

With regard to those of mixed Greek and Egyptian descent or of Hellenic education the evidence appears still more bewildering. In addition to the native beliefs which they had adopted they also maintained more or less intimate relations with the classic pantheon and dabbled in the syncretistic philosophy of Alexandria. The burials at Antinoë are typical of this class, and as we have seen the jumbling of religious ideas is astonishing. It is probable that amongst this class the gnostic teachers had most success, as its members had a smattering of Alexandrian ideas and were at the same time prone to the superstitions and belief in magic of the native-born. In examining these relics of early Christian communities scattered along the upper banks of the Nile we seem to be breathing in a very different atmosphere from that of Clement of Alexandria and the catechetical school. With the growth of power of the see of Alexandria and the suppression of gnosticism many of these irregular practices disappeared, but you may change a people's religion without changing their mental characteristics, and it is probable that the peculiar stamp always borne by Egyptian Christianity is to be traced back through this period to ideas long rooted in the past and ingrained in the very nature of the people

CHAPTER VI

EARLY CHRISTIAN ICONOGRAPHY IN EGYPT

THE question as to how far Christian iconography drew its original inspiration from pagan art will always be doubtful. It was several centuries before a definitely Christian art was evolved, and with the exception of certain symbols, such as the cross, the fish and the anchor, everything before the fourth century must necessarily be vague and uncertain. In Egypt, at least, Christianity began to be propagated at a time when the old native art was decaying and when hellenizing influences were already strong even in religious subjects. Superadded to this must be reckoned the curious current of influence introduced by Syrian motives which helped to effect the gradual change to the style that is termed "Byzantine[1]." It must be admitted that when the latter style predominated from the sixth to the eleventh centuries the Christian art and iconography of Egypt cut on the whole but a poor figure. It is however less in the style and art of Egyptian iconography than in its motives that we shall find our interest, while we shall only have recourse to the later Byzantine work when an illustration of the

[1] See Strzygowski, *Kleinasien ein Neuland der Kunstgeschichte*; also his *Hellenistische und Koptische Kunst*.

progress or persistence of a motive is desired. Also
where all is so vague, and much evidence is necessarily
of a dubious character, it will be better to discuss not
only designs which are admittedly Christian but also
those about which there is some doubt or controversy.

The oldest iconographical object in Egypt to which
a Christian origin has been assigned is undoubtedly a
gravestone now preserved in the museum of Cairo[1] and
first published by M. Gayet[2]. On it is seen rudely carved
in sunk relief a naked woman seated on a chair of ancient
Egyptian design suckling an infant: opposite her stands
a man in a Greek robe holding what appears to be a
palm branch in his right hand : above is the ancient
symbol of "heaven," and higher still can be seen the
drooping wings and claws of the vulture goddess.
There are also five incised vertical strokes which look
as if they had been intended to contain three lines of
text. On the back in Coptic characters is the short
funerary inscription of one Djakour and a peculiar
wheel-like cross. The block is of sandstone and
measures 1 ft. 9½ inches by 1 ft. 3½ inches. M. Gayet,
who was the first to point out this remarkable monument, apparently failed to notice the Coptic inscription
on the back. He, however, unhesitatingly considered
it a representation of the Virgin and St Joseph, and
described the former as " La Vierge assise sur le siège
d'Isis allaitant l'Enfant divin." Its date however he
considered to be after the council of Chalcedon when
in a revulsion from Greek or Byzantine influence the
Copts returned to the earlier art of their dynastic

[1] No. 8546.
[2] *Mémoires de la Mission arch. française au Caire*, III. 3, pl. XC.

ancestors. The theory of this return to original motives is certainly ingenious but quite impossible to fit in with the known facts. The late Dr Ebers was also much struck by this relief and agreed with M. Gayet as to its Christian origin. He went into some detail with regard to the figures, and pointed out the thoroughly heathen and old Egyptian style in which they were represented—the conventional Egyptian throne, the admittedly unchristian portrayal of the Virgin with bare breasts, her necklace and peculiar head-dress, and the resemblance of the child to the infant Horus—while he connected the vulture goddess of Nekhebit above with her character of protector in childbirth, regarding her, accordingly, as the protector of the Mother of God herself. He attributed the monument to the earliest period of *Coptic* art, and, like M. Gayet, saw in it an excellent example of the tendency of that art to return to the old native traditions[1].

Now if there is one thing certain about this object it is that it cannot be later than about the end of the second century and it is probably considerably earlier. Its style and technique stamp it unmistakeably as an example of the last stages of native art before it became absolutely moribund. The type represented full face and not in profile had already been known some time earlier, and examples may be found in the temples of the early Roman period in the Dodeka-schoinos and even in the Sudan. It is therefore evident that if this relief is of Christian design it must

[1] *Sinnbildliches, die koptische Kunst, ein neues Gebiet der altchrist-lichen Sculptur und ihre Symbole,* 1892.

be of the very earliest period, and can bear no relation whatever to the Coptic inscription on the back, which has every appearance of the fully developed script and could not be at the earliest older than the sixth century.

It is to Dr Carl Schmidt that we owe the true explanation of this relief[1]. It must be remembered that until he saw the original in the magazine of Cairo Museum the Coptic inscription on the back had escaped notice. To his surprise when he turned the stele over he found the words "The day on which Djakour fell asleep, Phaophi 8" in Coptic, which inscription he rightly assigns to the period between the 9th and 12th centuries. He further states that it is possible to recognize the sandstone as that peculiar to Erment, the ancient Hermonthis, which in Roman times was an important centre of the cult of Isis and Horus[2]. His contention that some tenth century Copt had taken an unfinished stele of the Roman period dedicated to the local cult of Isis and Horus and used it as a gravestone is incontestably correct. But the *provenance* "Erment" is exceedingly unlikely, for the reason that there is no sandstone in the immediate locality. The prevailing limestone characteristic of the Thebaid continues south beyond the town of Esna, so that there cannot be any "sandstone" peculiar to Erment. That the stele was originally made in some locality where Horus and Isis were particularly worshipped is very probable, but that locality must be sought further

---

[1] *Aegyptische Zeitschrift*, 1895, Vol. XXXIII. pp. 58 ff.

[2] Crum in his *Catalogue of Coptic Monuments* of the Cairo Museum assigns it to the neighbouring town of Esna.

south than Erment. The *provenance* therefore is
extremely doubtful, but may be Esna or Edfu.

, The next object of iconographical interest which we
have to consider is the so-called Horus St George in
the Louvre[1]. This is a granite group carved in high
relief, representing a hawk-headed man riding a horse
and spearing a crocodile which the horse tramples
under foot. It is, in short, a peculiar variation of the
representation of Horus spearing Typhon-Set in the
form of a crocodile. The god in this case wears the
garb of a Roman officer, a short skirt, a tight fitting
vest, and the *paludamentum* or military cloak over his
shoulders. He rides however without stirrups[2] and his
feet are bare. The chief peculiarity of this representation is the fact that Horus is mounted on horseback.
We have seen in a former chapter how important a
part Horus played in the mythology of Egypt as the
avenger of his father Osiris, a fact which led him to be
associated by the platonizing school of Graeco-Egyptian
Osiris worshippers as the emblem of rejuvenescence
conquering corruption and death, and the type of
Horus spearing the crocodile goes back at least as
far as the XVIIIth dynasty. In the Ptolemaic temple
of Dendera Set or Typhon is represented as a pig, but
otherwise the type remains the same. So it continued
into Roman times, and we have an example of Horus in
a similar attitude with his right arm raised and
wearing Roman military garb in a fine bronze in the

---

[1] First published by M. Clermont-Ganneau, *Revue Archéologique*,
1876, pp. 196 ff.

[2] Stirrups are unknown before the sixth century. See Forrer, *l. c.*,
and O. M. Dalton, *The Treasure of the Oxus*, p. 72.

British Museum[1] which may be approximately dated to
the 1st or 2nd century A.D.[2] All these types however
represent the god on foot and it must be admitted that
this relief is, so far, the only one that represents him
as mounted. It is perhaps the latest development
of the type and may probably be assigned to the third
century. The hawk's head has the appearance of the
local native work shortly after the close of the reign of
the Antonine emperors, when the old technique and art
began to fall rapidly off. The group too is obviously
an architectural ornament, as is evidenced by its deep
cutting and moulded frame, and the use of granite for
architectural and decorative purposes began to be
discontinued soon after this time[3]. At the end of the
third century granite was far too difficult a medium for
the clumsy stoneworkers that the Egyptians had by that
time become, and they confined their artistic skill
almost entirely to the plentiful and easily worked
lime- and sandstones. The dress of the warrior and
harness of the horse are unfortunately of little help as
guides to date, as such were worn until at least the time
of Constantine. The material and general appearance
of the relief are all we have to go on, but these are
sufficient to make it fairly certain that the date
suggested above is approximately correct.

M. Gayet, however, sees little difficulty in assigning
this monument to a time posterior to the Council of
Chalcedon. According to him this is St George slaying

[1] No. 36062.

[2] That the right arm was raised in this case and probably held a
spear is proved by the torso of a smaller statuette in the same attitude
also in the British Museum (No. 36051).

[3] Strzygowski, *Koptische Kunst*, pp. 8 and 80.

the dragon, and " ce retour vers l'association de la forme humaine est le gage le plus certain de la reviviscence du dogme ancien dans le dogme monophysite[1]." Apart from what has already been said in evidence of an earlier date, it may also be recalled that at the end of the fifth century, with perhaps the exception of the Isis cult at Philae, the worship of the ancient gods was dead.   Their names lingered on, it is true, but only in magical papyri as demons bound by the spells of magicians[2].   Nor is it clear as to how an animal-headed man is to typify the ancient doctrine and the mono-physite creed.   That some such form of representation might have been possible among the gnostics of the second or third century is conceivable, but to credit it to monophysite Copts is entirely to misunderstand the history and literature of the period.

There is however very much more likelihood of this object being the prototype not only of St George and the dragon but also of the military saints so dear to later Coptic art.   This was first pointed out by M. Clermont-Ganneau[3], who however was anxious to associate the group with Semitic mythology. Dr Georg Ebers also drew attention to a late Coptic stele in the Cairo Museum, on which is represented a military saint riding on a horse with a spear in his hand and what appear to be two antelopes in the field.   The work is very rude but is certainly reminiscent of the Louvre relief, and the same or a similar motive may be found in many of the Coptic representations of military

---

[1] *L'Art Copte*, p. 113.

[2] Erman, *Handbook of Egyptian religion* (Engl. edition), p. 228.

[3] *Loc. cit.*

saints. Unfortunately at present we have no complete chain of monuments which will link up the traditions of art without large intervening gaps, and until we have it is impossible to dogmatize. There is however little doubt that the older traditions did linger on, and it is quite conceivable that the origin of St George and the dragon is to be found in the Egyptian representations of the fight between Horus and Set.

These considerations lead very naturally to the question of the origin of the type best known as the "Madonna and Child." Unfortunately hitherto no early representation of this type has been found in Egypt, but it certainly appears in the Roman catacombs as early as the second century. Here in the oldest iconography the Virgin appears mainly under two types, the first representing her standing either alone or as one of a group of saints with the arms raised in the attitude of prayer, while in the second she is seated and holds the infant Christ on her knees. Of these the second is rarer, although there is good evidence to believe that the numerous figures of praying women or "orantes" in the catacombs are for the most part symbolical figures offering prayer for the souls of the dead and not figures of the Virgin as has sometimes been supposed[1]. To be noted here is a fresco of the Virgin and Child in one of the earliest Roman catacombs[2], and with it (a) a Ptolemaic bronze of Isis and Horus[3] and (b) a Graeco-Roman ivory Isis and Horus from

---

[1] Wilpert, *Cyklus christologischer Gemälde*, p. 30 ff.

[2] That of Priscilla. See Wilpert, *Malereien der Katakomben*, and Rossi, *Roma Sotterranea*, III., pl. CLXXVIII.

[3] *B.M.* No. 11131.

Egypt[1]. This last is remarkable, and before proceeding
with the discussion of the relation of these figures to one
another it deserves some passing notice.   At first sight
the object has an almost mediaeval appearance.   The
figure is seated on a throne clad in graceful and flowing
draperies, and her hair hangs in luxuriant locks on her
shoulders.   Only the legs of the infant seated on her
knees are left, the upper part of its body having been
broken away, but enough remains to show that the
child was naked.   But in spite of the general pose and
grace of the figure a closer inspection will render its
Isiac origin evident.   On the head of the goddess is a
head-dress like a *modius*, and if this is compared with
the crown (below the Hathor-horns and disk) on the
Ptolemaic bronze Isis its origin becomes at once clear.
Both are conventional representations of the circular
diadem formed of the heads of uraeus serpents, above
which was usually the solar disk and cows' horns of
Hathor[2].   The ringlets of the goddess recall the Roman
statue of Isis now in the Musée Guimet, and are similar
to those described in the ecstatic vision of Lucius[3].   Moreover the breasts are bare and the left hand is raised to
hold one towards the suckling infant.   The group is a
fine example of graceful Alexandrian work, and although
far removed from the conventional Ptolemaic prototype
its connexion with it is evident.

[1] *B.M.* No. 26255.

[2] The diadem of the ivory figure, which is without the disk and
horns (or possibly in this case the *atf*-feathers), is slotted on the top to
receive them, in the same way as is the diadem of the bronze Ptolemaic
figure.

[3] See *antea* p. 36.

Now if we turn to the seated Virgin and Child
group of the catacombs, the similarity of pose and
treatment cannot fail to be noticed. The Virgin it is
true wears no head-dress, but this is only natural as
the head-dress was part and parcel of the symbolism
of the heathen goddess. Her figure also is entirely
clothed, but otherwise the attitude and representation
are distinctly reminiscent of the Egyptian group. It
may be argued against this that any representations
of a woman seated with a child on her knees are bound
to be more or less similar, but there is one instance
at least in the catacomb frescoes which shows that
a completely different pose may be adopted[1]. It is
well known that the earliest Christians in Rome made
no scruple of using pagan designs and symbolism not
only in frankly heathen representations of nymphs and
goddesses but also as a groundwork for their own types,
as in the case of the " good shepherd " and so forth.
When moreover we consider that, at the time
Christianity was introduced into Rome, there were
several flourishing centres of the Isiac cult in Italy
where the modified Graeco-Roman symbolism of the
Egyptian religion would be frequent enough, it follows
that the probability of an Isiac inspiration is not so
slight as might be thought. It must be remembered
too that the technique and stylism of the Roman
catacombs were almost identical with those which
prevailed at Pompeii, where the Isis temple with its
frescoed walls was one of the most familiar and important buildings of the town. If, therefore, it is
legitimate to argue that the criophoric or moschophoric

[1] *Roma Sotterranea*, III., pl. CLXXVI.; *cf.* Wilpert.

figures of paganism were the prototypes of the "good shepherd," the Isiac origin of the Virgin and Child group is equally probable. This does not necessarily mean that the early Christians of Italy deliberately copied the Isiac group for one of their most sacred themes, or that they made direct use of a symbolism which was connected in their minds with what they considered the worship of devils, but rather that, in their art, they were influenced and allowed themselves to be inspired by a form of representation with which many of them were familiar.

In Rome the link which bound Christian with pagan art is painting and not sculpture. All the earliest decoration of the catacombs is through the medium of frescoes; sculptured reliefs did not come into vogue until a later period. As we have seen these decorations were freely inspired by pagan motives; but on this subject there are two main schools of opinion: (a) the apologists for a purely Christian art who maintain that the resemblance to pagan contemporary art is superficial and that we have here the seeds of an entirely new art which was eventually to revolutionize the world, and (b) those who see in the figures of the Good Shepherd, the prophets, virgins and martyrs, nothing but purely pagan designs. It is probable that the truth lies between these two extremes. At least with the representations of the Virgin and Child and of the Good Shepherd important modifications were introduced[1], although the pastoral scenes, the nymphs and fauns, Apollos etc. must be admitted to

[1] Veyries, *Figures Criophores: Bibliothèque des écoles françaises d'Athènes et de Rome*, Fasc. xxxix.

be purely pagan decorations. In Egypt however it is
far more difficult to trace the connecting link. Probably
the earliest Christian designs are those worked in
purple into the numerous specimens of cloth from
Akhmim[1]. Here we have nymphs and garlands among
which appear the cross and *swastika*, the fish and hare.
Again the decoration of coffins and funerary furniture,
which played so important a part in Egyptian art, may
very well have been the stepping stone by which pagan
symbolism was transferred to Christian decoration.
Oddly enough terra-cotta, the medium employed for
the representation of countless pagan deities, seems to
have been neglected by the early Christians of Egypt,
but one important exception to this appears in the
figure of the Good Shepherd found near Ahnas and
now in the Berlin Museum[2]. Although a rough figure
and not to be compared with the paintings of some of
the catacombs or the famous statue in the Vatican, it
follows closely enough the admirable description of
M. Veyries:

"Le Bon Pasteur a le costume des campagnards de l'époque.
Sa physionomie rustique, laide, vulgaire, mais honnête et douce,
sa tournure gauche, sa démarche lourde répondent à son vêtement:
c'est un paysan, un vrai berger, un homme de la classe misérable
que le Christ avait surtout aimée, qu'il était venu désigner à la
sollicitude à l'affection et à la prédilection du monde. Plus tard
seulement, quand l'Église sera libre et triomphante, il paraîtra
tout naturel de revenir au type élégant et jeune, imité de plus
près des figures païennes, dont les chrétiens, au lendemain de
la défaite du polythéisme, ne s'effrayaient plus comme d'impures
et dangereuses idoles[3]."

[1] See *antea*, p. 122.

[2] Nos. 14852 and 14866. Illustrated in Erman, *Handbook of
Egyptian Religion* (Engl. edition), fig. 117.

[3] *Loc. cit.* p. 79.

Our figure here represents a more Egyptian type than those of Rome.   His feet are bare, he has a shock of rough hair and he wears a *colobium* or coarse tunic. On his shoulders he carries the wandering sheep: he is represented as beardless and young.   According to Professor Erman[1] the figure was found among a number of pagan objects, but its Christian origin is indubitable. Its date is probably the early part of the third century.

An interesting design on a fragment of textile material from Akhmim represents a figure which is possibly that of the Saviour (Forrer, Taf. XVIII, No. 1). It is worked in white on a purple background and is probably to be attributed to the fourth century.   The scene shows a young man with curly hair, beardless, and wearing a long tunic and pallium.   In his left hand he holds aloft a cross and in his right is a cross-headed lance with which he spears a snake-like crocodile.   Forrer compares this figure with the half St George half Christ type of representation which was doubtless intended to symbolize the triumph of Good over Evil, of Christianity over Paganism, and this idea, he points out, is borne out by the figures of the eagle and the wolf worked above[2]. If this design from Akhmim represents Christ himself it is somewhat unusual, although the apparent youthfulness of the face is in no way remarkable, for this was a common form of portraiture in early times.   The bearded Christ seems to have been another and perhaps later tradition.   The figure may however only represent St George, in which case it is merely another version of what, as we have already seen, was a very common

[1] *Egyptian Religion*, p. 228.
[2] *Die frühchristlichen Alterthümer aus Achmim-Panopolis*, p. 28.

theme among the early Egyptian Christians, borrowed directly from the old religion.

It is possible also that we have other representations of Christ as the Good Shepherd from Egypt, for so at least Forrer would interpret two scenes woven on textile fabrics from Akhmim, which he also illustrates (Taf. xv, Nos. 1 and 2). On the left is seen a youthful beardless figure wearing a short sleeveless tunic and holding in his arms a lamb which he appears to be handing over to another similarly dressed figure who wears however a kind of gaiter on his legs. Lying down between the two figures is another lamb and in the upper right hand corner is a naked winged boy (?) who might possibly be taken for an angel. Now this may be merely a pastoral scene representing shepherds and their flocks with Eros in the background. It is clumsily executed and worked in bright colours, blue, green, and red, and its date is extremely hard to ascertain. Taking however into consideration the fact that it came from a Christian cemetery it is more likely to have a religious significance, and if Forrer's interpretation is right this little scene is of very considerable interest, for in it we have a very early iconographical representation of an important piece of early church symbolism. It is possible however that this explanation is pushed too far, although it is difficult not to be convinced that the scene represents the Good Shepherd and his flock.

Something has already been said of the smaller objects and representations hitherto found in Egypt chiefly from Akhmim and Antinoë, and these taken in connexion with the examples of iconography described in this chapter show what a very distinctive note characterizes the symbolism of the earliest Christian communities in the Nile valley. Although the style adopted was for the most part debased Graeco-Roman, it is certain that in some cases at least the idea that inspired the motive was taken from the old native religion. How far the old and the new faith blended on the borderline it is at present impossible to tell, but it is to be hoped that future excavations will render the interpretation of much that is now doubtful more certain, and that the dry all-preserving climate of Egypt will eventually allow a reconstruction of the life and customs of the earliest Christians from the actual documents and objects in use at the time.

CHAPTER VII

SOME ASPECTS OF GNOSTICISM: PISTIS SOPHIA

THE study of Gnosticism is made extremely difficult
not only by the inherently involved character of its
mysticism, but also by the unsatisfactory manner in
which the history of its doctrines has come down to us,
and it is at the best a somewhat dreary task. Until
a time comparatively recent our knowledge of the various
Gnostic sects was confined to the accounts given by
orthodox Fathers, among the principal of whom we
may cite Irenaeus, Hippolytus and Epiphanius. From
these were compiled more or less systematic histories
of the systems and doctrines of the Gnosis by
various investigators, chief among whom were Matter,
Mansell, Lipsius and Hilgenfeld, while the archaeological side was treated with much curious learning by
C. W. King, whose work was unfortunately marred by
inadequate knowledge of Egyptian cults. It was,
however, always felt that as long as dependence was
placed mainly on the descriptions given by the Fathers,
only an inadequate view of the subject was obtainable,
as the perspective was that presented by the foes of
the Gnosis and for that reason biassed and unfair.
Accordingly attention has more recently been turned
to actual Gnostic documents, which are, however,

exceedingly scarce. Several of these nevertheless have
survived, two of which may be reckoned as of first class
importance, namely the so-called Codex Askewianus in
the British Museum, better known as " Pistis Sophia,"
and the Codex Brucianus at Oxford containing the
" Books of Ieou," both of which MSS. came from
Egypt[1]. As a detailed discussion of Gnostic systems
would not be within the scope of this book, it will be
sufficient if we here confine our attention to the above
mentioned works, and their relation to Gnosticism in
general and Egyptian Gnosticism in particular.

The mysterious and involved speculations of the
different Gnostic teachers make it almost impossible to
arrive at the precise meanings of their various doctrines;
nevertheless a single philosophic thread seems to have
run through almost all of them in common. The
Supreme God was unknowable, unfathomable, and
beyond all human conception, the world having been
created by a Demiurge who was, according to some
sects, an imperfect emanation of the Supreme God.
Descending from the Demiurge was a vast concourse
of angels, aeons, and powers varying according as the
various sects drew their inspiration from Hebrew,
Zoroastrian, Egyptian or other sources, while the
spheres, heavenly, terrestrial and infernal, were marked
out into separate and distinct regions. In Christ many
Gnostics recognized the *Logos*, the representation of the
Supreme God, the Light whereby the mysteries of their
various and complicated systems were to be revealed,

[1] There are besides these and several magical fragments the works
known as *The Gospel of Mary*, *The Apocrypha of John*, and the
Wisdom of Jesus Christ yet to be published. It is understood that
Dr Carl Schmidt is engaged in editing them.

and accordingly his life and sayings were to be
particularly studied and revered. Nevertheless the
traditional life of Christ was regarded either as an
allegory or as a deliberate fraud which cloaked a
hidden meaning; the true revelation was only to be
obtained through the medium of an esoteric history
and doctrine not known to the ignorant and only to
be understood by the *illuminati* after a long period of
study and often of asceticism also. To those outside
the pale the early Gospel histories of Christ might be
sufficient; but to all who were willing to probe deeper
there was a mystic esoteric history and doctrine hidden
from the discernment of the vulgar, which gave the
key to all religions and philosophies and explained the
mysteries of the heights and the depths. The way in
which these mysteries were concealed in allegories,
manipulations of figures, employment of words with
occult meanings, and similar methods of obscurity,
afforded a great opportunity for mystics versed in the
various esoteric cults of paganism to build up around
the personality of Christ a mysterious doctrine the
intricacies of which are sufficient to make the brain
of the non-initiated reel.

There can be little doubt that Gnosticism made
great headway in Egypt during the greater part of the
second century. And this is what was to be expected.
Egypt had been a land addicted from time immemorial
to mysticism and magical practices, which were nevertheless of an eminently material character, wholly
lacking in any spirit of metaphysical speculation, while
in Alexandria, where were to be found men of all races
and creeds, religious syncretism had set in long before

the beginning of the Christian era. It is therefore not surprising that Christianity during its infancy, in a country where there were votaries of almost every conceivable cult known, and where the intellectual tendency was to build up a syncretism which would embrace all divergent creeds, should have been involved in the general *mêlée* of religious ideas. We know from the Fathers how powerful and numerous, especially in Egypt, were those who professed themselves Christians, yet who declared that Christianity was only part of the Light, and that the germ of the whole truth lay in all religions, but was only comprehensible to those who were initiated or were possessed of a mysterious *gnosis*. The earliest record of the conflict between those professing to expound the gnosis and the preachers of the simple gospel is the dispute between Paul and Simon Magus, the latter of whom appears to have been the first to associate Christianity with the Gnostic mysteries. From Palestine the esoteric cult quickly spread to Egypt by what has been called by King a kind of "counter-apostolic succession," and perhaps reached its height in the systems promulgated there by Basilides and Valentinus, although there is plenty of evidence to show that the doctrines were also widespread among the Christian communities of Syria and Asia Minor. Nevertheless it was in Egypt that these esoteric Christians flourished and were probably most numerous, and it is from Egypt that we are beginning to get direct evidence as to their systems and beliefs. Apart from engraved seals, gems and other small archaeological objects, we have now the beginnings of a Gnostic literature which has come down to us mainly through Coptic translations of the original Greek. The two most important of these works are, as has already been said, *Pistis Sophia* and *The Books of Ieou*.

The MS. of the work known as *Pistis Sophia* was sold by its original owner Dr Askew to the British Museum towards the end of the eighteenth century, and with the exception of the notice by Woide[1], who was the first to draw attention to it, the MS. received little or no examination by scholars. The language employed is Coptic[2], but recourse has been had to the frequent employment of Greek words where the Coptic had no equivalent for expressing mysterious and involved ideas. It is generally agreed by Coptic scholars that the work is a translation from a Greek original or originals, and that the Greek words were merely transcribed by the translator. Woide by comparing the MS. with the writing of the Codex Alexandrinus came to the conclusion that its date was to be assigned to the fourth century. A copy made by him of the text presumably came later into the hands of Münter, a Danish bishop, who published a treatise on it[3], and some thirty-five years later still an article by Dulaurier appeared on the subject[4]. It was not, however, until 1851 that a proper edition of the MS. appeared, a work

---

[1] *Beiträge zur Förderung theologischer und anderer wichtigen Kenntnisse*, Vol. III. p. 55. Kiel und Hamburg, 1778. See also Woide's *Appendix ad editionem Novi Testamenti Graeci e codice MS. Alexandrino*.

[2] The dialect is Sahidic.

[3] *Odae Gnosticae Salomani tributae, Thebaice et Latine, praefatione et adnotationibus philologicis illustratae.* Havniae, 1812.

[4] *Journal Asiatique*, Vol. IX. 1847, p. 534.

undertaken by Schwartze, who published the Coptic text with a Latin translation. Schwartze unfortunately died before his labours were complete, but the work was finished by his friend Petermann, and this remained for many years the standard edition[1]. Schwartze's publication may be said to have given a fresh impetus to Gnostic studies, for since it appeared, *Pistis Sophia* has occupied a very important place in every work dealing with Gnosticism. Apart from these it has since received fresh treatment by itself from the hands of Amélineau[2], Harnack[3], and Schmidt[4]. It is to the laborious and careful investigations of the last named that the present writer and all future workers in this obscure field must owe a great debt. Mention may also be made of a careful English translation made from Schwartze's and Amélineau's editions for the benefit of Theosophists by Mr G. R. S. Mead, which although written from a modern mystic's standpoint contains in the preface a good account of the literature on the subject[5].

Pistis Sophia is not a self-contained work but a miscellany. The codex falls into four distinct divisions, of which the first has no title. The second division is

[1] *Pistis Sophia opus gnosticum Valentino adjudicatum.* Berolini, 1851.

[2] *Pistis Sophia ouvrage gnostique de Valentin, traduit du Copte en Français* (Les classiques de l'Occulte), Paris, 1895.

[3] *Über das gnostische Buch Pistis Sophia*, Leipzig, 1891.

[4] *Koptisch-Gnostische Schriften. Die Griechischen-Christlichen Schriftsteller der Ersten 3 Jahrhunderte*, Leipzig, 1905; also *Gnostische Schriften in Koptischer Sprache aus dem Codex Brucianus. Texte und Untersuchungen zur Geschichte der Altchristlichen Literatur*, Vol. VIII. 1892.

[5] *Pistis Sophia*, London, 1896.

headed by the words "The Second Book of Pistis Sophia," but this is an addition of a later hand and the title should be, according to Schmidt, the words found appended at the end of the division, *i.e.* "A portion of the Books of the Saviour." In the middle of the second division appears what is obviously an interpolation consisting of the fragmentary conclusion of a book on the "Mystery of the Ineffable," thus forming a third division, while the fourth part again has no title. This last is a distinct work and has nothing in common with the rest; Schmidt is inclined to see in it the conclusion of an apocryphal gospel. The first three divisions form a more or less connected whole which may be divided into two parts, the first of which deals with the fall of Pistis Sophia ("Faith-Wisdom") and her restoration through the thirteen aeons to her former position, while the second contains a number of questions put by Mary and some of the disciples to Jesus concerning the highest mysteries, the Mystery of the Ineffable, and the Mystery of Mysteries, and the explanations offered by the Lord in reply. In any case the title by which the book has become generally known is not really correct, as Pistis Sophia plays the principal rôle in only a limited portion of the work. A better title would be according to Schmidt "The Book of the Saviour," or according to Harnack "The Questions of Mary and the Disciples concerning Repentance and Forgiveness and the answers of the Lord." The whole compilation seems therefore to have more of the character of a series of extracts from what must have at one time been the works of a single Gnostic sect. But before considering its date, *provenance*, and authorship it will be well to give a brief summary of its contents.

The first part of the book commences with a statement that Jesus had passed eleven years after his resurrection discussing and explaining to his disciples the esoteric mysteries: the more important and mysterious of these have however not yet been divulged, and they are now to be imparted with their due interpretations and meanings. The scene is accordingly laid on the Mount of Olives, where Jesus appears to his assembled disciples "on the fifteenth day of the month Tybi, the day of the full moon[1]," transfigured by a glory of exceeding great light in which he ascends to heaven before their astonished eyes. He passes through the regions of heaven, where all the powers that dwell there became confused and amazed at his appearance, and "all the angels with their archangels and all the Powers of the Height all sang from the Inmost of the Inmost so that all the world heard their voice." "On the ninth hour of the morrow" he descends again in great glory to his disciples, but they are unable to support the greatness of the light which transfigures him, and he at their request draws the light within himself. At this point the actual teaching commences. Jesus begins by explaining the mystery of his own Incarnation, and the origin of John the Baptist and of the disciples themselves, in the following words. "It came to pass that when I had

---

[1] Usener (*Weihnachtsfest*, p. 20) has pointed out in this connexion that the 15th of Tybi was the date on which, according to Clement (*Stromateis*, l. 21, § 146), certain Basilidian sects observed the festival of the Saviour's baptism.

come into the midst of the Archons of the Aeons
I looked out upon the world of mankind at the
command of the First Mystery, I found Elizabeth the
mother of John the Baptist before she had conceived
him, and I sowed in her a power which I had taken
from the little Iaô the good, who is in the midst, that
he might thereby preach before me and prepare my
way and baptize with water of the forgiveness of sins.
That Power then is in the body of John. And further,
in the region of the soul of the Archons which he is
destined to receive I found the soul of the prophet
Elias in the Aeons of the Sphere, and I took him out
and took his soul and brought it to the Virgin of Light,
and she gave it to her Receivers, who brought it to the
sphere of the Archons and then cast it into the womb of
Elizabeth. And the Power of the little Iaô, who is in
the midst, and the soul of Elias the Prophet are united
in the body of John the Baptist." This is intended as an
explanation of the saying "It is written in the Scripture
that when Christ shall come Elias will come before
him and prepare his way." Jesus then continues: " It
came to pass after this that I looked upon the world
of mankind at the command of the First Mystery, and
found Mary who is called my mother according to the
material body : I spoke to her in the form of Gabriel,
and when she had turned to the Height towards me
I placed in her the first Power which I had taken from
the Barbelo[1] that is the body which I bore in the
Height. And instead of the soul I cast into her the

---

[1] Perhaps the most likely of the originals offered for this name is
that of Matter (*Histoire critique du Gnosticisme*, 1827, II. 280)
בַּעְלָא] בְּרַת־בַּעְלוֹ [?], *Daughter of the Lord*.

Power which I had received from the great Sabaoth
the good who is in the region of the Right; and the
twelve Powers of the twelve Saviours of the Treasure
of Light, which I had taken from the twelve Ministers
who are in the midst, I cast into the Sphere of the
Archons. And the Decans of the Archons and their
Liturgi thought that they were the souls of the
Archons; and the Liturgi brought them and bound
them in the bodies of your mothers; and when your
time was fulfilled you were born into the world without
the souls of the Archons being in you."

Following this explanation of the esoteric origin of
himself and the twelve apostles, the Saviour next dis-
courses of his three mystic Vestures. The first of these
bore the words *zama zama ôzza rachama ôzai* the interpretation of which is said to be : " Oh Mystery which is
beyond the World that thereby all may exist: this is the
whole Outgoing and the whole Rising which has caused
to emanate all Emanations and all that is therein.
Because of it all mysteries and all their places exist[1]."
The first vesture contained " the whole glory of all the
names of all the mysteries, and of all the emanations
of the orders of the spaces of the Ineffable." The
second " the whole glory of the name of all the mysteries, and of all the emanations which are in the order of
the two spaces of the First Mystery." The third vesture
contains " The glory of the name of the Mystery,
of the Revealer which is the first commandment,

---

[1] These five words are, of course, a jumble of some Hebrew or
Aramaic jargon. I would suggest צמח meaning a "shoot" or "scion,"
a word sometimes used for the Messiah, as the origin of *Zama*, and the
other three may perhaps be interpreted " strength, mercy and might."

and of the mystery of the five impressions, and of the mystery of the great ambassador of the Ineffable, which is the great Light, and also of the mystery of the five Leaders who are the five supporters. And moreover there is also in that Vesture the glory of the name of all the orders of emanations of the Treasure of Light with their saviours, and of the mystery of the order of their orders, which are the seven amens and the seven voices and the five trees and the three amens and the Saviour of the Twins which is the Child of the Child, and of the mystery of the nine guardians and the three gates of the Treasure of Light. And moreover there is in it all the glory of the names of all who are on the right and in the midst. And there is further in it the whole glory of the name of the Great Invisible who is the Great Forefather, and the mystery of the three triple powers, and the mystery of all their places, and the mystery of all their invisibles and of all those who are in the thirteenth Aeon, and the name of the twelve Aeons and of all their Archons and of all their archangels and of all their angels and of all who are in the twelve Aeons, and every mystery of the name of all those who are in the ' *Heimarmene* ' and in all the heavens, and the whole mystery of the name of those in the spheres and in their firmaments, and all that they hold and their regions."

The Saviour is next represented as relating how on obtaining this vesture he traversed the twelve Aeons, after having passed the gates of the Firmament and the spheres of Fate. In each of these Aeons dwell a number of Powers, " all the angels of the Aeons, their archangels, their archons, their gods, their lords, their authorities, their tyrants, their powers, their sparks, their stars, their unpaired, their invisibles, their forefathers, and their triple powers," who on seeing the light of Jesus "were thrown in confusion against one another, and great fear fell upon them when they saw the great light that was in me. And their great confusion and great fear reached to the region of the great invisible Forefather and the three great Triple Powers." Having thus narrated the power he obtained, presumably by the possession of his mystic vesture, over the principalities and powers of the Spheres and the Aeons, the Saviour tells his disciples how he altered the position of the fates and spheres belonging to the Tyrants of the Aeons, and how he took away a third of their power. Especially did Adamas, the Great Tyrant, fight against the light. This rebellion against the light is then further expounded in great detail on the questioning of Mary and Philip. When this is complete, we come for the first time to the mention of the Power named Pistis Sophia, who has given her name to the work.

According to the narrative the Saviour found Pistis Sophia in the thirteenth Aeon. Her position had apparently aroused the jealousy of the rulers of the twelve other Aeons, because she was above their mysteries. Accordingly Arrogant (*Authades*), a sinister power, caused to emanate from himself a lion-faced power in Chaos, and this latter exercised a fatal fascination on Pistis Sophia, who forsook her own place and after being angrily chased through the twelve Aeons lost her light and fell into Chaos. Being in great misery in Chaos she appealed to the Light of Lights in a prayer

of repentance, whereupon she is restored to the Aeons
She then traverses in succession the twelve Aeons, and
at each of the twelve steps she makes a prayer of
repentance and an appeal against the lion-faced power
and other powers that restrain her. Each of these prayers
is offered by the Saviour for interpretation to a disciple,
and each is explained by long passages from the
Psalms. Jesus then continues the narrative, saying
that he finally sent forth a great Light Power who
restored Pistis Sophia to the thirteenth Aeon, and her
song on this occasion is interpreted by Salome from
the Odes of Solomon. After Pistis Sophia has sung
another song the mystery of the Light Power who
came to her rescue is explained, and then comes a very
curious narrative.

"And Mary answered and said My Lord, concerning
the word that thy power prophesied through David
Mercy and Truth are met together, Righteousness and
Peace have kissed one another ; Truth hath flourished
on the earth and Righteousness hath looked down
from heaven.' So hath once thy power of this word
prophesied concerning thee. When thou wert little,
before the spirit came upon thee, while thou wert
with Joseph in a vineyard, the spirit came from the
height and came to me in my house, like unto thee,
and I recognized it not and thought that it was thou.
And the spirit spoke to me and said ' Where is Jesus
my brother that I may meet him ? ' And when he
said thus to me, I was in doubt and thought it was a
ghost tempting me. I took him then and bound him
to the foot of the bed in my house, until I had gone
out into the field and found you, thee and Joseph, in

the vineyard where Joseph was putting up vine props.
It came to pass then that when thou didst hear me
speaking to Joseph thou didst understand what I said,
and went joyfully and saidst ' Where is he that I may
see him, rather did I expect him in this place.'   It
came to pass then when Joseph heard thee say this he
was troubled, and we went back together, entered the
house and found the spirit bound on the bed.   And
we gazed on thee and found that thou wert like him;
and when that which was bound on the bed was loosened,
he embraced thee and kissed thee and thou didst kiss
him and ye became one.'"

This very interesting piece of magic is interpreted at
some length by Mary as the twofold essence of Christ
meeting in his earthly body; Mercy being the spirit
sent from on high by the first Mystery, and Truth the
power which issued from Barbelo; and so forth in
similar strain.   A variant interpretation is also offered
later in the meeting of Mary and Elizabeth, the mother
of John the Baptist.   At this point the first part ends
somewhat abruptly with the note of a scribe added in
a later hand.   Not to be outdone in the mysticism
he had been reading, he wrote: "These are the names
which I will give of the Infinite.   Write them with a
sign that the sons of God may be hereby manifest.
This is the name of the Immortal One, AAA, ωωω.
And this is the name of the Voice whereby the Perfect
Man has been moved, III.   And this is the interpretation
of the name of this Mystery: the first which is AAA,
its interpretation is ΦΦΦ; the second which is MMM
or ωωω, its interpretation is AAA; the third which
is ΨΨΨ, its interpretation is OOO; the fourth which

is ΦΦΦ its interpretation is NNN; the fifth which is ΔΔΔ, its interpretation is AAA. He who is on the throne is AAA: this is the interpretation of the second; AAAA, AAAA, AAAA; this the interpretation of the whole name."

The narrative is taken up again in the so-called "Second Book," with a further interpretation of "Mercy and Truth have met together etc.," by the disciple John. Jesus then continues his exposition of the restoration of Pistis Sophia, describing how he despatched, on the command of the First Mystery, a light-stream to her by the hands of the archangels Gabriel and Michael. This light-stream restored the Light Powers to Pistis Sophia, and its effect is interpreted by Peter from one of the Odes of Solomon beginning "A flood hath come to pass; it hath become a great stream strong and wide; it hath carried everything away etc." Pistis Sophia is then again attacked by Adamas and his emanations, and again illuminated by a light-stream brought by Michael and Gabriel. Finally Jesus narrates how "by order of my Father, the First Mystery who looked within, I myself went down into Chaos shining exceedingly, and turned against the Power with the lion-face who shone exceedingly and took from him all the Light that was in him, and held fast all the emanations of Arrogant so that they cannot from now enter into their region which is the thirteenth Aeon. And I took away the Power from all the emanations of Arrogant and they all fell back into Chaos powerless....And I led Pistis Sophia forth from Chaos, and she trod on the emanation of Arrogant with the serpent's face, and also on the seven-headed basilisk emanation, and she trod on the lion-faced Power, and the dragon-faced. I made Pistis Sophia stand upon the seven-headed basilisk, emanation of Arrogant, for it was mightier than all in its wickedness. And I, the First Mystery, stood by it and took all the powers which were in it and destroyed all its matter so that no seed should arise from it henceforth." An interpretation of this is then offered by James from the psalm (xc.) "Whoso dwelleth under the defence of the Most High shall abide under the shadow of the God of heaven." The work then continues by Jesus narrating a series of songs sung by Pistis Sophia to the Light, each of which is interpreted from the Odes of Solomon or from the Psalms by Mary, Martha or one of the disciples, until Pistis Sophia is finally restored to the thirteenth Aeon by the Saviour.

Hereafter the theme of the narrative changes somewhat, and Pistis Sophia drops out. Mary Magdalene is represented as questioning the Saviour on the mysteries and receiving long expositions of esoteric teaching. The subjects explained include the twenty-four Invisibles, the Regions of the Rulers of Fate, the twelve Aeons and the thirteenth Aeon, the regions of the Midst and the Right, the Treasure and its twelve Saviours and their "ascension," also concerning the powers Ieou and the great Sabaoth, and the sealing of the souls of the perfect. The questioning is then taken up by John, to whom the Saviour describes the "absolute mystery" and what that mystery knows. The *gnosis* is very extensive, and includes nearly everything in the seen and unseen world, knowledge of all of which is guaranteed to the person who shall

11—2

know this mystery.   Quite what it is is not explained, but the Saviour says of it: "Whoso shall renounce the whole world and all that is therein and shall submit himself to the Godhead, that mystery shall be simpler than all the mysteries of the kingdom of light, and it is easier to understand than all and simpler than they all.   He who shall arrive at the knowledge of this mystery, has renounced the whole of this world and all the cares that are in it.   Wherefore, my disciples, be not sad thinking that ye will never understand that mystery.   Verily I say unto you that mystery is far simpler to understand than all the mysteries, and verily I say unto you that mystery is yours and also his who shall renounce the whole world and the matter that is therein."   Proceeding, the Saviour explains that the mystery of the Ineffable is in all other mysteries, and he then relates of the power received by the soul after death if it knows the mysteries, he who dies without the *gnosis* being in a parlous state *unless those who know the mysteries utter them over him*[1], in which case the wretched uninitiated soul is hurried through the regions of torment and thus escapes punishment. Further, concerning the lower mysteries, Jesus says that they may be found "in the two Books of Ieou which Enoch wrote when I spoke with him from the tree of knowledge and the tree of life which were in the Paradise of Adam."   There follows an exhortation to purify themselves for the reception of the mysteries by renouncing the world and all that is in it.

At this point the concluding words of a lost book are inserted concerning the dignity of the "members

[1] See pp. 173, 174.

of the Ineffable" and the blessedness of those who are initiated into the mysteries.

Jesus is then represented as continuing his teaching, ordering the disciples to preach renunciation of the world, and a long catalogue of sins to be renounced is recited, including, oddly enough, "superstition." This code is extremely severe, and the punishments in Amenti that are to be the reward of these sins are terrible. There is therefore little doubt as to the high morality inculcated in this extraordinary work, and this is intensified by a command to be loving and merciful to all men and to minister to the sick and poor. Mary is then represented as questioning Jesus as to the fate of the initiated and uninitiated at death. The righteous among the latter are quickly and mercifully passed through the regions of torment and sealed by the Virgin of Light, after which they are sent back into the world again, according to the type of sins they have committed, with further opportunity of obtaining the light of initiation. For those who receive the mysteries hypocritically the "jaws of the Dragon of outer Darkness" are reserved. The rules concerning the fate of the initiated who have sinned but who repent, vary in degree, but the progress through the regions of torment to the Virgin of Light will be hastened by the celebration on their behalf of the "third mystery of the Ineffable." The friends of the dead are to say "Set ye free the soul of such and such a man of whom we are thinking in our hearts, free him from all the torments of the Archons and hasten him quickly to the Virgin of Light; in that month may the Virgin of Light seal him with a lofty seal, and in that month let the Virgin of Light cast him into a body that shall be righteous and good, that he may enter into the height, and inherit the Kingdom of Light." "And if ye say these words, verily I say unto you that all who are in the ranks of the judgment of the Archons hasten to pass that soul from one to another until they send it to the Virgin of Light. And the Virgin of Light sealeth it with the sign of the kingdom of the Ineffable and giveth it unto the Receivers, and the Receivers will cast it into a righteous body, and it will find the mysteries of light so that it will be good and go up and inherit the kingdom of Light." Moreover the initiated will be enabled to soar aloft into the light after death without waiting in the regions of the Archons. At this point, it says, the disciples "became frenzied" at the sublimity of the doctrines the Saviour teaches.

There follows an exposition of the constitution of man. From this it appears that man, besides a soul, possesses a counterfeit spirit ($\dot{a}\nu\tau\dot{\iota}\mu\iota\mu o\nu\ \pi\nu\epsilon\hat{v}\mu a$), and while the soul is ever seeking after the region of Light and the whole Godhead, the counterfeit spirit drags down the soul and constrains it ever to sin. The Saviour then relates how the souls of the sinful are haunted by the counterfeit spirit after death until they are given new birth and new opportunities, but the souls of the righteous who are possessed of the knowledge of the mysteries become radiant light-streams which ascend to the region of their mysteries. Those possessed of the mysteries, but sinful, suffer in various degrees according to their repentance, while he who is possessed of the mysteries in the first mystery

and is still unrepentant, "his dwelling is in the midst
of the jaws of the Dragon of Outer Darkness, and last
of all he shall be frozen up in torments and lost for
ever," while those who have received the mystery of
the Ineffable and remain unrepentant are doomed to
annihilation for eternity.   After some further account
of the various treatment of various sinners, and a pro-
nouncement on the infinite compassion of the First
Mystery illustrated by a trial of Peter's compassion,
we come to a gap in the MS.   This is followed by a
description of the regions of torment.   The Outer
Darkness is a great Dragon with its tail in its mouth,
which surrounds the whole cosmos : within it are the
places of judgment and twelve dungeons, there being
an Archon in each dungeon, the face of which Archon
differs from that of each of his fellows.

"The first Archon in the first dungeon is crocodile-faced and
it has its tail in its mouth.   Its authentic name is Enchthonin.

"The Archon in the second dungeon ; its authentic face is
a cat's : it is called in its region Charachar.

"The Archon in the third dungeon; its authentic face is a
dog's: it is called in its region Acharoch.

"The Archon in the fourth dungeon ; its authentic face is a
serpent's: it is called in its region Achrochar.

"The Archon in the fifth dungeon; its authentic face is a
black bull's: it is called in its region Marchour.

"The Archon in the sixth dungeon; its authentic face is a
boar's: it is called in its region Lamchamor.

"The Archon in the seventh dungeon ; its authentic face is a
bear's: it is called in its region by its authentic name Luchar.

"The Archon in the eighth dungeon ; its authentic face is a
vulture's: it is called in its region Laraoch.

"The Archon of the ninth dungeon ; its authentic face is a
basilisk's : it is called in its region Archeoch.

"And in the tenth dungeon are many Archons, each of them

in its authentic face has seven dragons' heads; and he who is over them all is Xarmaroch.

"And in the eleventh dungeon, in this region also, are many Archons, each of them with authentic faces has seven cats' heads; and the great one over them is called in their region Rochar.

"And in the twelfth dungeon there are also many Archons, a great multitude, each of them in its authentic face with seven dogs' heads; and the great one that is over them is called in their region Chremaor.

"These Archons, then, of these twelve dungeons are inside the dragon of Outer Darkness, and each has a name for every hour and each of them changes its face every hour. And each of these dungeons has a door which opens to the height...and an angel of the height watches at each of the doors of the dungeons....And the dragon of Outer Darkness has twelve authentic names which are written on its doors, a name for the door of every dungeon; and these twelve names are all different from one another, but all twelve are contained one in the other so that he who uttereth one name will utter all."

It then further appears that, although the torments in the dragon of Outer Darkness are described as terrible, they may be avoided (1) by the uninitiated who repent, and (2) by the initiated who have neglected the mysteries. In the first case the friends of the dead man are told by the Saviour to "celebrate the one and only mystery of that ineffable which ever forgiveth sins," and when the celebration of that mystery is finished, "Amen I say unto you, if the soul for which ye shall pray is in the dragon of Outer Darkness, it shall take its tail from out its jaws and let that soul escape." In the second case "All who shall obtain the mystery of one of the twelve names of that dragon of Outer Darkness, even though they be sinners and should have previously received the mysteries of the light and then have sinned...such men if they pass out of the body without again repenting, and if they have been carried into the torments which are in the belly of the dragon of Outer Darkness...such, if they know the mystery of one of the twelve names of the angels during their life while they are in the world, and then pronounce one of their names when they are in the midst of the torments of the dragon, then, the moment when they shall pronounce it, the whole dragon will be shaken and will be thrown into the greatest anguish, and the door of the dungeon in which the souls of such men are will open above, and the ruler of the dungeon in which they are will cast the souls of such men out of the belly of the dragon of Outer Darkness, because they have discovered the mystery of the name of the dragon." Jesus then proceeds with an exposition of the occult system of gestation and the embryonic stage of the soul, which from the first is dogged by the " counterfeit spirit" ever seeking to drag it down to evil. Finally he explains that the mysteries are for all men and that some are in the Books of Ieou, that none of the prophets or the patriarchs or any before himself had received the mysteries, but that all those righteous souls who lived before his Incarnation would be sent back again into righteous bodies to find the mysteries of the light.

The last book of all, as has already been said, has no connexion with what precedes it. Its most interesting point is that it contains apparently a description of the celebration of an ineffable mystery for the remission of sins. It opens by saying that the disciples came to Jesus on the third day after the crucifixion beseeching his mercy. " Then Jesus stood with his disciples by the water of the Ocean and pronounced this prayer, saying :

'Hear me my Father, thou Father of all fatherhood,
endless light *aeaiouo iao, aoi, oia, psinother, thernops,
nopsither, zagoure, pagoure, nethmomaoth, nepsiomaoth,
marachachtha, thobarrabau, tharnachachan, zorokothora,
ieou sabaoth*[1].' And while Jesus said this, Thomas,
Andrew, James, and Simon the Canaanite stood in the
west with their faces turned to the east. Philip and Bar-
tholomew stood in the south facing to the north; and
the rest of the disciples with all the women disciples
stood at the back of Jesus. But Jesus stood at
the altar. And Jesus cried out, turning to the four
corners of the world with his disciples who were all
clad in linen robes, and said : *iao, iao, iao.* This is the
interpretation thereof: *Iota,* the All has gone forth;
alpha, they shall return within; *omega,* there shall be
an end of ends." "And when Jesus had spoken this he
said '*iaphtha, iaphtha, mounaer mounaer ermanouer
ermanouer,*' that is to say 'Thou Father of all fatherhood of endlessness; hear me because of my disciples
whom I have brought before thee that they may believe
in all the words of thy truth; grant unto them all

[1] In the case of these mystic names a venture may be made to
give a derivation of some of them, but only with the greatest diffidence.
The first four words of this prayer are variations on the vowels
supposed to express the Supreme God, so dear to the Gnostics.
Psinother, as has already been suggested by Amélineau (*Gnosticisme
égyptien,* p. 320) is Egyptian for "the son of God," [but its original
must have been *Psh^ere-nouter,* not the old-fashioned *Psa-nouter* as
given by Amélineau], *thernops* and *nopsither* being variations of the
same word. *Marachachtha* may, perhaps, be מרקחתא, "unction," a
reference to the Messiah, *thobarrabau* is probably אתא בר רבא, "Thou
art the Son of the Great One," while *tharnachachan* may be a corruption of אתא רחמנא, "thou art merciful." *Zorokothora* is Persian and
was a word in use with the Manichaeans; *ieou sabaoth* is יהוה צבאות,
"Lord of Hosts."

things for which I have cried unto thee, for I know
the name of the Father of the Treasure of Light.'
Again did Jesus, that is to say Aberamentho, cry out
pronouncing the name of the father of the Treasure of
Light and said : ' May all the mysteries of the Archons
and the rulers and the angels and archangels and all
the powers and all things of the invisible God *Agram-
machamerci* and the Barbelo and the Bdella withdraw
themselves and betake themselves to the right.'   And
in that hour all the heavens moved to the west, and all
the Aeons and the Spheres and their Archons and all
their powers flowed together to the west, to the left of
the disk of the sun and the disk of the moon.   And
the disk of the sun was a great dragon with its tail in
its mouth mounted on the seven powers of the left, and
drawn by four powers in the likeness of white horses.
But the basis of the moon was like a ship which a
male and female dragon steered and two white oxen
drew ; the figure of a child was on the stern part of the
moon, who steered the dragons which seized the light
from the rulers ; and at its prow was the face of a cat.
And the whole world and the mountains and seas sped
to the west to the left.   And Jesus and his disciples
remained in the midst of an aerial region in the path
of the way of the midst which lies below the Sphere,
and they came to the first order of the way of the
midst.   And Jesus stayed in the atmosphere of his
region (*i.e.* the way of the midst) with his disciples."

Jesus then describes in a briefer and more concise
manner than in the foregoing books the system of the
Aeons and their rulers and the infernal spheres and
their rulers.   The upper spheres correspond to the

divisions of the zodiac, while amongst the rulers of the
various regions are found the names of all sorts of
deities, Kronos, Ares, Hermes, Aphrodite, Zeus, Paraplex, Hekate and Typhon. Aphrodite is also called
Khosi and the Ram of Bubastis, while a female monster
called "Aethiopic Ariouth" plays a considerable rôle
in the infernal hierarchy. Following on this the
disciples are witnesses of a beatific vision in which fire,
water, wine and blood have a mystic signification.
The scene then changes to the "Mount of Galilee,"
where the esoteric sacrament before mentioned is
performed by the Saviour.

"And Jesus said to them [the disciples] 'Verily
I say unto you, not only will I cleanse your sins but I
will make you worthy of the kingdom of my father;
and I will give you the mystery of the forgiveness of
sins upon earth, whereby those whom you shall forgive
on earth shall be forgiven in heaven, and he whom you
shall bind on earth shall be bound in heaven. I will
give to you the mystery of the kingdom of heaven that
you yourselves may transmit it unto men.'

"And Jesus said to them, 'Bring me fire and vine
branches.' They brought them to him; he set the
offering and placed two wine-jars one on the right
and the other on the left of the offering. He placed
the offering in front, and put a cup of water before the
wine-jar on the right and a cup of wine before the
wine-jar on the left, and laid bread according to the
number of the disciples between the cups and placed
a cup of water behind the bread. Jesus stood before
the offering, and placed his disciples behind him all
clad in linen robes, and in their hands was the number

of the name of the Father of the Treasure of Light. And
he cried out saying, ' Hear me O Father of all fatherhood,
endless light. *Iao, Iouo, iao, aoi, oia, psinother, the-
ropsin, opsither, nephthomaoth, nephiomaoth, marachachtha, marmarachtha, ieanamenamau, amanei* of
heaven, *israi, amen, amen, soubaibai, appaap, amen,
amen, deraarai* behind, *amen, amen, sasarsartou, amen,
amen, koukiamin, miai, amen, amen, iai, iai, touap,
amen, amen, amen, main, mari, marie, marei, amen, amen,
amen*[1]. Hear me O father of all fatherhood. I invoke
you also ye forgivers of sin and cleansers of iniquities.
Forgive the sins of the souls of these disciples and
make them worthy to be reckoned in the kingdom of
my Father, the Father of the Treasure of Light, for they
have followed me and kept my commandments. Now,
therefore, O Father of all fatherhood, let those who
forgive sins draw nigh; these are their names : *siphireps-
nichieu, zenei, berimou, sochabricher, euthari, nanai,
dieisbalmerich, meunipos, chirie, entair, moathiour,
smoar, peucher, oouschous, minionor, isochobortha*[2]. Hear
me when I call upon you, forgive the sins of these souls
and blot out their iniquities. May they be worthy to

---

[1] The first twelve words of this invocation have already appeared (see
p. 170). *Ieanamenamau* is perhaps a play on the word *amen* with vowel
variations. *Amanei* looks like a form of the old Egyptian god's name
Amen. Israi = Israel. *Soubaibai* (with great diffidence) = Egyptian
"soul-star" or "star of the double hawk." *Appaap* = Syrian egyptian-
ized "Father of Fathers," or else the old Egyptian demon *Apap.*
Sasarsartou = סַר־סָרְדְיוֹטוֹת (= στρατιώτης with Hebrew plural), an
Aramaic Greek equivalent of יהוה צבאות (cf. Dalman, *Aramäisch-
Neuhebräisches Worterbuch*, p. 287); *mari, marei, marie* = variations of
the Syrian word מרי "Lord."

[2] The present writer is unable to suggest any derivations for these
mysterious syllables.

be reckoned in the kingdom of my father, the Father of the Treasure of Light, for I know thy great powers and invoke them, *aner, bebro, athroni, eoureph, eone, souphen, knitousochreoph, mauonbi, mneuor, souoni, chocheteoph, choche, eteoph, memoch, anemph*[1].'....And it came to pass that the sign which Jesus had spoken was given. Jesus said unto his disciples, 'Rejoice and be glad for your sins are forgiven, your iniquities blotted out, and ye have been reckoned in the kingdom of my father.' When he had said this the disciples rejoiced with great joy."

Jesus continues by authorizing his disciples to perform this mystery for the forgiveness of the sins of others. He then speaks of another mystery, a baptismal sacrament, and further of the power possessed by those who know the Name which is higher than all and contains all names. This Name uttered to any Archon, archangel, angel, principality, power, or demon of the outer darkness renders the utterer complete master of any opposition. The work ends finally with a description of the torments of the wicked in Amenti, the most interesting point being that not only are the ordinary sins of the world enumerated for punishment, but also unnatural vice and the foul and filthy rites of some of the other Gnostic sects which were so severely condemned by the fathers.

The above is a brief *résumé* of *Pistis Sophia*, a work of considerable length and extraordinary complexity. As to its date, we have not only to consider that of the Coptic MS. itself, but, what is more important, the

[1] I am again unable to explain the meanings of any of these magical words. *Choche* may possibly be Eg.="darkness."

Greek originals from which the Coptic scribe drew. There has been considerable divergence of opinion concerning the date of the Coptic codex, Amélineau dating it as late as the ninth or tenth century[1], while Schmidt considers the fifth century more probable[2]. The latter is the most likely date. The Greek original, however, is considerably earlier, and its date has been discussed in detail by Harnack, who produces several very cogent reasons for assigning the original or originals of the work to the second half of the third century[3]. With this Schmidt agrees[4], adding that he thinks that the fourth part, which differs considerably from the rest and contains the account of the celebration of the mystery, may be placed half a century earlier. There can be little doubt that Schmidt's surmise is correct, as in the last part the *gnosis* is less involved and has not yet become so elaborate as in the earlier parts. It may be therefore said with some degree of certainty that the whole work may be assigned to the third century, the first parts probably to the second half and the last part to the first. Greater divergence of opinion is evident when we come to consider the sect of gnostics from which *Pistis Sophia* originated. Koestlin[5], Lipsius[6], Jacobi[7] and Harnack[8] have argued for an Ophite origin, but as our knowledge of this sect is of a very hazy character it does not help the unravelling of the problem to any great extent.

[1] *Pistis Sophia.* Introduction, p. 9.
[2] *Koptisch-Gnostische Schriften*, p. 13.
[3] *Über das Buch Pistis Sophia*, p. 95 ff.
[4] *Loc. cit.* p. 17.   [5] [*Theolog. Jahrbuch*, 1854.]
[6] See art. Gnostics, *Dictionary of Christian Biography*.
[7] [Herzog's *Real-Encykl.* (2nd Ed.), v. p. 244.]   [8] *Loc. cit.*

Amélineau[1] has accepted without hesitation the authorship of Valentinus himself or of one of his disciples;
a Valentinian origin had also been put forward by
several earlier scholars, including Woide[2], Dulaurier[3],
Schwartze[4], and Renan[5]. But the authorship or inspiration of Valentinus was strongly opposed by Schmidt,
chiefly on the ground of the scarcity of known Valentinian elements in the work[6]. Both Schmidt and
Harnack come to the conclusion that *Pistis Sophia*
was the work of the sect known from Irenaeus as the
" Barbelo-gnostics," a large group of Syrian origin
embracing the smaller sects of Nicolaites, Ophites,
Cainites, Sethians and Archontics. But if of Syrian
origin the scheme betrays here and there marked
signs of Egyptian influence, and the fact that the work
was sufficiently important to be translated[7] into the
native tongue shows without doubt that the sect which
inspired it was an Egyptian branch who dwelt in Egypt.
As, however, the Egyptian side of *Pistis Sophia* is that
which concerns us most it will be well to discuss it in
some detail.

Amélineau, in his work *Le Gnosticisme égyptien*,
not only strongly favours a Valentinian origin for
Pistis Sophia, but goes farther and declares that one

[1] *Loc. cit.*

[2] [*Appendix ad editionem Novi Testamenti Graeci e Codice Alexandrino*, Oxonii, 1799 ; cf. Harnack, *Pistis Sophia*, p. 35.]

[3] *Journ. asiat.*, 1847.   [4] *Pistis Sophia*, 1851.

[5] *Marc Aurèle*, p. 120 f.   [6] *Gnostische Schriften*, p. 557 ff.

[7] This point, put forward by Schmidt, may be pressed too much.
The Coptic text is at the earliest a fifth century work when gnosticism
was fast dying out and could only be practised furtively. How little
the Copt who translated *Pistis Sophia* understood of what he was
writing is shown by his blunders and mistakes.

of the main sources of Valentinus' inspiration was the ancient Egyptian religion, a theory which he seeks to establish by connecting many of the doctrines attributed to Valentinus with the doctrines of the old Egyptian religious system. It must be confessed, however, that few of his parallels are convincing. The old Egyptian religion is so protean that a general resemblance could be ransacked from somewhere amongst its many conflicting beliefs to match vaguely almost any doctrine of any religion. It must also be borne in mind that to draw parallels, as M. Amélineau does, between the doctrines of the XVIIIth and XIXth dynasty texts and those of Valentinus is highly unsatisfactory, as in the interval of 1500 years the religion of Egypt had become greatly changed; moreover, as we have already seen in a former chapter, religious decay and want of knowledge concerning the ancient beliefs were already widespread in Valentinus' time. Even supposing a Valentinian origin for *Pistis Sophia*, the evidence of a close acquaintance with the old Egyptian doctrines in that work is entirely lacking. It is true that its general connexion with the customs of Roman Egypt is established by the use of the Egyptian calendar (the 15th of Tybi is several times specified), by the occurrence of the barbaric names few of which nevertheless are of purely Egyptian origin, that are frequently found on the magic papyri of the time, and by the opposition offered to the filthy and obscene rites performed by certain so-called gnostics who, according to Epiphanius, flourished particularly in Egypt. Harnack has also pointed out that the Odes of pseudo-Solomon so prominent in *Pistis Sophia* were most probably composed in Egypt[1], but they have nothing to do with the native religion. So that although in these we have several undoubted points of close contact with the general mixed religious character of Egyptian thought at that period, we have at the same time nothing that can be said to be of specifically native inspiration among these facts except perhaps a few garbled names. There are, however, several important exceptions, which nevertheless show not how well the author was acquainted with the old beliefs, at least in their unhellenized form, but how very little he really knew about them.

The most striking example of a direct connexion with the native religion is the description of the dragon of Outer Darkness and his twelve dungeons of torment each with a gate and guarded by a monster. This is undoubtedly directly inspired by the old Egyptian Duat with its twelve divisions separated by gates each full of demon-headed beings, and it is the more likely to be so when we consider that the beliefs concerning the Duat or Tê remained practically unchanged in the Roman period, as is shown by the story of Si-osiri and Setne Khaemuas. Whether the dragon of Outer Darkness is to be identified with the arch-fiend Apap is more doubtful. But although the author of this description of the regions of torment drew his inspiration from purely native sources, those sources must either have been hopelessly corrupt or he understood them only very slightly. Not only is the name of the guardian of each dungeon entirely un-Egyptian, but also the author has described the

[1] *Über das Buch Pistis Sophia*, p. 41 ff.

animals usually represented in scenes of the underworld without understanding them properly. Although
the majority may be recognized easily enough as gods
of the Duat, no such creature as that with a boar's or
bear's head ever appeared in that region, or indeed in
the whole range of Egyptian mythology, while that
having the face of a cat should be more properly
described as with the face of a lioness. Again, we
have another image purely inspired by native Egyptian
iconography, that of the "basis" of the moon. This is
said to be "like a ship whose helms were a male dragon
and a female dragon, drawn by two white oxen. The
figure of a babe was on the poop steering the dragons...
and at the prow was the face of a cat." Now the lunar
Thoth or moon god is frequently represented in a bark,
and the steering paddles of these divine barks had
handles usually carved to represent hawks' heads, a
near enough parallel to the dragons of *Pistis Sophia*.
The babe on the poop, however, is clearly meant for
the figure of Harpokrates sometimes found seated on
the sterns of *solar* ships in these quaint representations.
That these divine barks were drawn in sacred processions by oxen is also quite probable. The face of
a cat at the prow, however, is never found. We are
therefore forced to the conclusion that the originator
of *Pistis Sophia* had only a scanty acquaintance with the
native religion of Egypt, or else derived his knowledge
from some corrupt source such as the Graeco-Roman
cult of Isis, which had by this time departed a long
way from the ideals and ritual of its native original.
It is therefore extremely unlikely that a philosopher,
such as the composer of *Pistis Sophia* must have been,

who so curiously garbles his only direct reference to
Egyptian mythology, should have any knowledge of
the religious ideas of the eighteenth and nineteenth
dynasties.

Perhaps the most remarkable trait of *Pistis Sophia*
is the strong sacramental element running through it,
which has been brought out in so interesting a way by
Harnack[1]. *Pistis Sophia* teaches that Christ is not
only the medium through which the mysteries of the
gnosis may be learnt, but he is also the all-compas-
sionate Saviour explaining how by the performance of
certain sacraments forgiveness of sins may be obtained
and the punishments of the wicked after death may be
lessened or remitted. In the first three parts of the
work these sacraments are only hinted at and not
explained, but in the last we have an actual exposition of one of these sacraments. That its ultimate
foundation rests on nothing more than the repetition
of a magical formula does not lessen its interest for
us, for as Harnack points out this Gnostic sect anticipated by many years the doctrine of sacramental
efficacy afterwards developed by the Roman Church.
He says, "In this respect *Pistis Sophia* is a document
of the first rank ; for we possess no second work which
places before our eyes so clearly the pre-history of the
Catholic sacramental doctrine as this Coptic work.
We meet here in a sudden appearance and at one
blow among the gnostics at the end of the third
century what the Catholic church worked out pain-
fully and slowly in the succeeding centuries. This
Gnosticism is not the father of Catholicism, but rather

[1] *Loc. cit.* p. 95 ff.

an elder brother who attained by storm what the younger brother acquired in the following period through a thousand troubles[1]."

We may consider a final point that should be of interest to us in this connexion. It is perhaps to this or some similar Gnostic system of sacramental efficacy that some of the unusual funerary customs among the early Christian communities in Egypt may be traced. We have seen how the excavations in the cemetery of Antinoë showed that wine jars and baskets of bread were buried with the dead, and both here and in the oasis of Kharga many tombs were constructed with small chapels at the entrance, as if for the celebration of some ceremony for the benefit of the deceased. *Pistis Sophia* tells us that mystical sacraments carried out by the friends of the dead procured not only forgiveness of sins, but also a swift passage through the regions of torment or the Aeons and the Spheres; it therefore seems natural that where the gnostics should congregate, there they should perform these sacraments for their dead. Water, wine, and bread formed the most important elements in these sacraments according to *Pistis Sophia*, so that earthenware vessels and baskets might naturally be found in their tombs. Moreover, it must be remembered that the will of Aurelius Colluthus found at Antinoë expressed the wish that the holy offerings might be celebrated for the repose of his soul, and although this will is no earlier than the first part of the fifth century it certainly displays a strong belief in sacramental efficacy. We may even bring the extraordinary mummies from Deir el-Bahari under our view

[1] *Loc. cit.* p. 114.

in this connexion.   The wild syncretism of *Pistis Sophia*
makes the scene representing the bark of Seker on their
robes less improbably Christian, while it strengthens
the sacramental evidence of the wine-cup and wheat,
if wheat it is, held in the hands of the deceased[1].

[1] See *ante*, p. 126.

CHAPTER VIII

THE BOOKS OF IEOU AND OTHER
GNOSTIC FRAGMENTS

THERE are three other works of interest and importance that emanated originally from the same sect as that which produced the *Pistis Sophia* writings. They are the two *Books of Ieou* and an unnamed fragment of some length from a gnostic work closely related to the others. They are written in Coptic in two hands, one according to Dr Schmidt of the fifth, the other of the fifth to sixth centuries. These form the so-called Codex Brucianus brought back from Egypt by the celebrated Scottish traveller James Bruce and acquired by the Bodleian Library in 1842. Like *Pistis Sophia*, the codex was copied by Woide, who was therefore the first to draw attention to it, and he used the information he thus gleaned in his version of the Coptic New Testament[1]. At a later period Schwartze copied Woide's copy and collated it with the original, but death prevented him from producing an edition of the text. This was left to M. Amélineau, who after giving several short extracts[2] produced an edition[3], which however received

---

[1] *Appendix ad edit. N. T. e Cod. Alex.*, 1799.

[2] *Annales du Musée Guimet*, Vol. xiv. p. 249 ff. and *Revue de l'histoire des religions*, Vol. xxi. 2, p. 175 ff.

[3] *Notices et Extraits des MSS. de la Bibliothèque nationale et autres Bibliothèques*, Vol. xxix. Pt. 1.

very severe criticism at the hands of Dr Carl Schmidt[1]. Finally Dr Schmidt succeeded in completing an edition which, considering the difficulties presented by the disorganized and faulty condition of the MSS., is a triumph of patient and critical study[2].

The two "Books of Ieou" which form the first part of the Codex were not only in a hopelessly confused condition with regard to the arrangement of their sheets, but were mutilated also by several long gaps. The first book is headed by what Dr Schmidt thinks is a motto, "I have loved you and wished to give you life. Jesus the living is the knowledge of Truth," and then goes on "This is the Book of the knowledge of the Invisible God by means of the occult mysteries." The theme of the opening passages is the saying attributed to Jesus "Blessed is he who hath crucified the world and not allowed the world to crucify him... He who hath crucified the world is he who hath found my word and hath fulfilled it according to the will of him who sent me." Jesus is represented as saying this to the assembled apostles; he continues with an explanation of the way in which evil may be overcome by a diligent acquisition of occult and hidden knowledge. This explanation has not gone very far when it is broken off by a large gap in the MS., and when we are able to take up the thread again we find ourselves plunged into a stereotyped account of the 60 emanations of Ieou, 28 of which only remain. Each of these is illustrated by a diagram showing its "mark," its

---

[1] *Götting. gelehrte Anzeigen*, No. 17, 1891, No. 6, 1892.

[2] *Gnostische Schriften in Koptischer Sprache aus dem Codex Brucianus*, Vol. VIII. *Texte und Untersuchungen*, Leipzig, 1892.

"name," its "guardians," and its "emanations." This part of the book is an explanation of the esoteric doctrine in a systematized form, and it is probable that it is to its extraordinary contents that allusion is made in *Pistis Sophia* as the "lower mysteries described in the Books of Ieou." Another large gap renders this system incomplete, and the MS. is next occupied with a description of the journey of Christ with his disciples through the 60 "Treasures," only seven of which remain owing to the mutilated condition of the MS. Here again the mystic name and seal of each is given to the disciples by Jesus, and the seal is illustrated by a diagram. This is followed by a hymn to the "unapproachable God." This is full of mysterious names and strings of apparently meaningless vowels and consonants. At the conclusion are the words "The Book of the great κατὰ μυστήριον λόγος," which Schmidt thinks should be the title of the whole work.

The second treatise is perhaps of greater interest and bears a very close relationship to the last part of *Pistis Sophia*. The scene is probably laid, according to Schmidt[1], in Judaea, and Jesus is represented as imparting to the twelve male and female disciples, in the twelfth year after his ascension, the greater mysteries which have hitherto been withheld from all men. It is important to note that by carrying out these mysteries Jesus declares that the souls of the dead are taken by the "receivers" of the Treasure of Light, cleansed of all sins, and brought through all the "regions" to the Treasure of Light: in other words the regions of torment may be avoided by the performance

[1] *Gnostische Schriften*, p. 326.

of the mysteries. Nevertheless only those are worthy to receive the mysteries who have renounced the world and all its goods; the disciples themselves have fulfilled this obligation by forsaking father and mother and all. Especially unworthy are those who indulge in filthy and obscene rites under pretence of esoteric knowledge. In short asceticism is the key to the mysteries. Before all these mysteries however he promises to give to them the three mystic baptisms: the Baptism by Water, the Baptism by Fire, and the Baptism by the Holy Ghost, and also to impart the mystery of spiritual unction. He who shall know these mysteries must become sinless, and shall thereby overcome the evil influences of the Archons. At these words the disciples are represented as becoming sore troubled, and they fall weeping at the feet of Jesus, beseeching him to impart to them the mysteries of the Treasure of Light in order that they may pass into those regions after death. Jesus has mercy on them and promises to reveal to them also the mystery of the Treasure of Light which is the mystery of the nine Guardians, of the three doors of the Treasure of Light and the manner of calling them, the mystery of the Child of the Child, of the three Amens, of the five Trees, of the seven Voices, and of the Wills of the forty-nine Powers, of the great Name of all Names, that is of the Great Light which surrounds the Treasure of Light. These are the highest mysteries, and, if performed once, all sins from childhood to death are blotted out. The soul of such a one so equipped becomes the heir of the kingdom of God and passes through all the Aeons and all the regions of the mystic spheres unhindered.

We then come to the celebration of the three baptisms. Jesus sends his disciples to Galilee to obtain from the hands of a sinless man or woman two wine jars and branches of vine. The man or the woman must be pure and virgin. When these are brought he prepares an offering, placing one wine jar on the right and one on the left, and places incense and various spices over all. The disciples stand near clad in white linen robes, wearing olive wreaths on their heads, in their mouths a fleawort bloom, and in their hands the cipher of the seven Voices. After turning to the four corners of the world Jesus utters a prayer to the "Father, the Father of all fatherhood, endless Light" which opens with mystic and apparently meaningless words, and continues by praying that the fifteen handmaidens of the seven Virgins of Light may baptize the disciples with the water of life and blot out their sins. If the Father hear his prayer Zorokothora Melchisedek will turn the wine in one of the jars into the water of living baptism. The miracle is duly performed: the wine in the jar on the right is turned into water and the disciples are baptized; they partake of the offering and are sealed.

The Baptism of Fire follows. Jesus constructs a pile of various incenses and spices, spreads a linen robe over the place of offering, and sets out a jar of wine and pieces of bread according to the number of the disciples. These stand in the same manner clad in white, with the cipher of the seven Voices in their hands, but this time wearing wreaths of dovewort. Jesus utters a prayer similar to the foregoing, after turning to the four corners of the world, and requests the forgiveness of his disciples' sins. If the prayer is to be answered he asks that Zorokothora Melchisedek will bring the water of the Baptism of Fire of the Virgin of Light. The miracle is duly performed, Jesus baptizes his disciples, seals them, and gives them of the offering.

The third Sacrament is precisely similar. The disciples wear white linen and myrtle wreaths. Jesus sets two wine jars and bread according to the number of the disciples, he utters a mystic prayer asking the forgiveness of their sins, calls on Zorokothora Melchisedek to perform his miracle, baptizes the disciples and seals them on the forehead with the cipher of the Virgin of Light. They partake of the offering.

Jesus then performs the mystery by means of which the disciples may overcome the hostility of the Archons of the Aeons. He places on the ground vine branches and various incenses. The disciples wear garlands of wormwood, lay incense on their lips and carry the cipher of the three Amens in their hands. Jesus offers another long prayer to the Father beseeching him to remove the tyranny and hostility of Sabaoth Adamas and his Archons from the disciples. So may they become immortal and follow Jesus through all the heavenly spheres wheresoever they will.

Jesus then explains to his disciples the "Apologies" of all the regions, their Mysteries, Baptisms, Offerings, Seals, Receivers, Ciphers and True Names, so that they may, equipped with this knowledge, pass through them all at will. He explains how the soul, equipped with the mystery of the forgiveness of sins, will pass through the rank of the three Amens, the Child of the Child,

the Saviour of the Twins, the Sabaoth of the Treasure
of Light, of the Iao the good, of the seven Amens,
the five Trees, the seven Voices, the Achoretoi, the
Aperantoi, Prohyperachoretoi, Prohyperaperantoi, Ami-
antoi, Prohyperamiantoi, Asaleutoi, Hyperasaleutoi,
Apatores, Propatores, five Charagmai of Light, three
Choremata, five Parastatai, the triple Spirits and triple
Powers of the Great King of the Treasure of Light, of
the First Command, of the Inheritance of Silence and
Peace, and of the Curtains that hang before Ieou
himself, the great King of the Treasure of Light.
When the mystery of the whole Treasure of Light has
been fulfilled and the mystery of the forgiveness of
sins, then Ieou permits the soul to enter his kingdom
and all the regions of the Great Light.   The soul then
penetrates through the door of the second Treasure
of Light where are the twelve great Powers which the
True God emanated from himself.   In this region a
great light-power will be given by the True God to
the twelve disciples, which will not only prevent them
from falling back, as was the fate of the unfortunate
Pistis Sophia, but will carry them farther to the
Treasure of the True God, who will give them a great
seal, a great mystery, and a great name.   The True
God will call to the Unapproachable God who will
send a light-power who in turn will give them the
mark of the seal of the Treasure of the True God,
and in that Treasure they will remain in everlasting
bliss.

Jesus then promises to give them the mystery of
the forgiveness of sins, that they may become Children
of Light, and acquainted with all the mysteries of the

celestial spheres.   He propounds the seals and their
names, the ciphers, the names of the Archons and their
"apologies."   The Archons will betray the utmost fear
of anyone knowing these mysteries and will immediately
allow a free passage to the person so illuminated.   At
this point the text breaks off and the rest of the work
is missing.

Appended to the MS. are two fragments of gnostic
prayers and a short fragment of a treatise concerning
the passage of the soul through the Archon of the
Region of the Midst.   These belong to the same sect
which evolved *Pistis Sophia* and the Books of Ieou, but
are probably somewhat later in character.   They all
find close parallels in passages of *Pistis Sophia*[1].

One of the first things which becomes obvious to
the student of the Books of Ieou is their close
resemblance to *Pistis Sophia* both in language and in
style ; while the second of the two books of Ieou can
only be a longer and more detailed account of the
mystic sacrament performed by Jesus in the final
section of *Pistis Sophia*.   We meet in both works the
same mystic names and ideas, so that there can be little
doubt that the two works originated from the same sect
or circle of gnostics.   This sect as we have already seen
was probably the so-called Barbelo-Archontic school,
which appears from these two works at least to have
been strongly tinged with the ascetic ideals prevalent
in many of the religious systems of the time and
finding powerful advocates in the Church itself among
the Encratites.   There can also be little doubt as to
the date of the Greek original of the Books of Ieou :

---

[1] See Schmidt, *Gnostische Schriften*, p. 24.

it must have been composed in Egypt about the same time as *Pistis Sophia*, that is to say during the first half of the third century.

The first treatise of the Books of Ieou contains a purely systematic arrangement of the various mysteries of the heavenly worlds, aided by diagrams which are all explained to the disciples by Jesus. This is followed by a more speculative discourse intended to be a means by which the initiated may overcome the different "Treasures," and to this end their seals, names, and ciphers are revealed. Both the systematic and speculative sections are brought together concisely by the concluding hymn. The importance of the second treatise lies in its strong advocacy of sacramental efficiency. The three most important sacraments described are the Baptisms by Water, by Fire, and by the Holy Ghost, but there is some reason to suppose that these mysteries are not only baptismal but also have a eucharistic character[1]. In each case there is made an "offering" of which the disciples partake in company with Jesus, and in one case pieces of bread (as in *Pistis Sophia*) are laid out according to the number of the disciples. It would thus appear as if the sacraments were a combination of both baptismal and eucharistic symbolism. Their importance in connexion with the forgiveness of sins thereby in securing a speedy passage through the aeons to the higher world of light cannot be overrated; and again we may perhaps trace many of the curious burial customs revealed at Antinoë, and possibly the extraordinary symbolism depicted on the shrouds of the Deir el-bahari mummies,

[1] This is not the view of Schmidt; see *Gnostische Schriften*, p. 491 ff.

to this anxiety of the gnostics to insure for themselves an everlasting and esoteric felicity by performing mystic sacraments.

Again, the Books of Ieou, and in a lesser degree *Pistis Sophia*, bear an outward resemblance to the purpose aimed at by such Egyptian works as the Book of the Dead, the Book of what is in the Duat, and kindred works. These were intended to be "guides" to a world beyond the grave, and regarded in this light they have a close resemblance to this circle of gnostic literature. In both the other worlds there were regions hostile to the passage of the soul, and the object of both classes of work is to prepare the soul by means of esoteric knowledge to overcome the powers of these hostile regions. Strange to say, the "magic" in certain cases is based on the root idea common to all magic of this class, the idea that if the soul were informed as to the *name* and other minute particulars belonging to the hostile power, it by that means acquires complete control over the unfriendly power, and is able to break down all hostility. But when we come to examine the details of the gnostic works, there is very little evidence of a close inheritance from Egyptian native religious ideas, the general scheme being evidently descended from the systems of the Syrian mystics. There is of course the notable exception of the specifically Egyptian symbolism of the twelve dungeons of the underworld, of the bark of the moon, and of the counterfeit spirit described in *Pistis Sophia*. But even in the more systematic Books of Ieou it is difficult to grasp what the system really is. There seems to be no definite explanation with which the reader is supposed to be well acquainted. Schmidt indeed, in opposition to Amélineau, thinks that the two Books of Ieou are in no way complementary to one another and are unconnected by any continuous current of thought. Indeed only one point is common to the two, and to *Pistis Sophia*, that Jesus makes these expositions to his disciples in the twelfth year after his resurrection. This last of course may be an arbitrary idea of the author's. In any case it is probable that both *Pistis Sophia* and the Books of Ieou may only be compilations from earlier and more complete gnostic works, and form a kind of compendium of the esoteric mysteries.

The remaining treatise which occupies the last part of the Codex Brucianus differs somewhat remarkably from *Pistis Sophia* and the Books of Ieou. Unfortunately both the beginning and end are missing, but it is nevertheless a treatise of some length. It is in short a thoroughly systematic account of the evolution of the esoteric world and its powers, in which a certain Setheus plays an important part. Contrary to the manner in which the other gnostic works imparted their mystic instructions by putting their doctrines into the mouth of Jesus and his disciples, there is in this work no mention either of Jesus or of sacraments or rites: the author simply gives an account of the birth and evolution of the transcendental world. Schmidt has found among its bewildering doctrines and the strings of names of the various powers several very definite clues by which the identity of the originating sect may be ascertained with some certainty[1]. In the first place Setheus, he points out, is the Greek form

[1] *Koptisch-Gnostische Schriften*, p. 25.

of the Old Testament Seth, who was held in great
reverence as an authority by the sect known as the
Sethians. Again the four great luminaries, Eleleth,
David, Oraiael and another missing in this work, are
cited by Irenaeus[1] as important beings in the Barbelo-
gnostic system, and the names of the Aeons, also given
by him in his work against the gnostics, Autogenes,
Monogenes, Logos, Christos, Adamas, etc., appear again
here. The reference to Marsanes undoubtedly connects it with the account given by Epiphanius of the
Archontians[2], in which he says that the Archontians
"declare that there are also other prophets, Martiades
and Marsianos, who were snatched up to heaven and
after three days came down again." Schmidt holds
that Marsanes and Marsianos are identical. Again the
mention of Nicotheos in our work recalls the reference
by Porphyry[3] to an "apocalypse of Nicotheos" in use
among the gnostic school of Aquilinus and Adelphius
which flourished in Rome during the middle of the
third century. This sect belonged more specifically
to the Sethian-Archontic group which produced the
Apocalypse of the Allogenes, "the Allogenes" being,
according to Epiphanius[4], another name for Seth. The
Archontics used seven books of Seth and seven books of
the Allogeneis, the last being the sons of Seth. Putting
this evidence together, Schmidt is of opinion that this
work belongs to the Sethian-Archontic group of gnostics.
Its early date, *i.e.* about 170–200, he no longer maintains,
but ascribes it now more probably to the first half of the
third century. If the Nicotheos referred to in the work

---

[1] Irenaeus I. 29. 2.   [2] *Heresies*, 40. 7.

[3] *Vita Plotini*, c. 16.   [4] *Loc. cit.*

is the same as the Nicotheos of Plotinus and Porphyry
this later date must be more correct. Although the
topography of the heavens and the speculation about
the transcendental world are fantastic in the extreme,
the main influences at work are Syro-hellenic and there
is little evidence of Egyptian influence. Schmidt thinks
that there can hardly be any doubt that it was ex-
cogitated on Egyptian soil, but it seems more probably
to have been an importation at some early period in
the history of gnosticism, possibly from Rome itself.

Before concluding this brief survey of early gnostic
literature a very interesting magical spell may be recalled which has distinct affinities to the works produced
by the circle of gnostic sects we have been discussing.
It will be remembered that magical spells of every kind
had always found great acceptance with the Egyptians,
and some examples displaying the extraordinary syncretism characteristic of the epoch with which we are
dealing have already been given in a former chapter[1].
It can be readily seen that such fantastic speculations
as those of the gnostics would provide excellent material
for the magician and dealer in black arts, but it is perhaps
not an altogether curious thing that the magician as a
rule makes such a garbled hash of his spells that their
origin is almost impossible to divine. So far nothing
that can be definitely attributed to any particular
gnostic sect has been found, although magical papyri
and amulets exist in considerable numbers. This spell,
however, is distinctly reminiscent of the Barbelo-gnostic
tenets. It comes in the middle of the long collection
of spells which forms the great magic papyrus now in

[1] See pp. 126, 182.

the Bibliothèque nationale at Paris[1] and is interesting
to philologists also as a jumble of Greek and Coptic.
The words present one of the oldest examples of Coptic
palaeography. The spell, which may be dated according
to Wessely[2] about the year 300, runs as follows[3]:

"A good method for casting out demons : Invocation to be
said over his (the afflicted's) head ; throw in front of him
branches of olive.

"Hail God of Abraham ; hail God of Isaac ; hail God of Jacob.
Jesus Christ, the holy, and the spirit, the son of the father who
is above the seven and within the seven. Bring Iao Sabaoth,
that thy power may mock at that until thou hast driven away[4]
the unclean demon Satan who is upon him. I exorcise thee,
demon, whoever thou art, by this god, Sabarbathiot, Sabarbathiouth, Sabarbathioneth, Sabarbaphia. Come out, demon,
whoever thou art and leave such a one. Now ! Now ! Come
forth at once demon, as I bind thee with adamantine and
unbreakable bonds and give thee over to the black chaos among
the lost."

There follows a short ceremony which includes the
tying together of seven olive branches.

Now the appeal made in this charm is to Iao
Sabaoth, a corruption of course of the Hebrew " Jahweh
of Hosts," and it may be recalled that two of the most
beneficent powers in *Pistis Sophia* are Iao the good and

---

[1] Wessely, *Sitzungsberichte der K. K. Akademie der Wissenschaften*,
Vol. xxxvi. p. 27.

[2] *Les plus anciens monuments de Christianisme*, p. 184.

[3] The text is difficult and has been the subject of elucidations,
besides that of Wessely, by Erman (*Ä. Z.* xxi. 1883. 3) and Griffith
(*Ä. Z.* xxxviii. p. 93, 1900). A copy of the text was published by
Mr F. Legge (*P.S.B.A.* May 1897, pp. 183–187) with a restoration and
translation. Mr Crum made (*P.S.B.A.* 1898, p. 102) some corrections
of Mr Legge's text and gave a satisfactory explanation of some of
the more obscure words.

[4] Reading with Wessely, *loc. cit.*

Sabaoth the good, whether in their greater or lesser form. Again the mystic number seven which occurs so frequently in *Pistis Sophia* and the Books of Ieou, *e.g.* the seven Amens, the seven Voices etc., may perhaps find an echo in the words of the charm "the father who is above the seven and within the seven," while the ceremony of placing olive branches before the possessed recalls the ceremony of setting out vine and other branches in the mystic sacraments. This charm of course is what may be classed as illegitimate magic; it is at least a magic of a lower order than that of the mystic sacraments, and as is usually the case with these exorcist charms, it contains only a garbled collection of mystic names and ideas. Nevertheless it seems to belong to the same family as the *Pistis Sophia* literature and for that reason may perhaps be classed with it[1].

[1 As a further example of the continuance of gnostic ideas in magic (much degenerated) during Coptic Christian times may also be quoted the interesting spell published by Mr Crum in his *Catalogue of the Coptic Papyri in the British Museum*, No. 1008 (MS. Or. 5987), from which we excerpt the following passage: "Pantokratôr Iaô Sabaôth Môneus Soneous Arkôeous (?) Adonai Iaô Elôi, who is in the Seventh Heaven and judgeth the evil and the good: I conjure thee today, thou that providest for me the twenty thousand demons which stand at the river Euphrates, beseeching the Father twelve times, hour by hour, that He give rest unto all the dead." Iaô Sabaôth here = the Deity (Jehovah): "the throne of Iaô Sabaôth" is mentioned in another passage of the spell.]

CHAPTER IX

THE RISE OF CHRISTIAN ASCETICISM
AND MONASTICISM

UP to now we have been dealing with the elusive
aspects presented by the more irregular and unorthodox
sections among the early Christians, who aimed by
judicious blending and mystic interpretations at forming a syncretistic connexion between Christianity and
the pagan systems in vogue. But at the time these
gnostic sects were evolving their esoteric mysteries a
movement had been begun among the more regular
Christians that was destined to become of world-wide
importance. The actual practice of asceticism and the
ascetic ideal was, as we have seen, older than Christianity,
but it appears to have affected the new religion almost
from the first[1]. The Encratite movement within the
church of Alexandria had for its aim the interpretation
of the teaching of Christ as a system of rigid self-denial
and abstinence from the ordinary pleasures of life.
Glimpses of this movement we have already found in the
fragments of certain apocryphal gospels discovered in
Egypt and discussed in a former chapter. How far the
movement was connected with the asceticism practised
not only by the platonizing Jewish communities of

[1] See Zöckler, *Askese und Mönchtum*, 1897, pp. 149–192.

Therapeutae but also by the devotees of the platonized
cult of Isis and Osiris it is difficult to say, but it is
probable that this philosophic ideal of purity and self-
denial influenced the early Christians in the same way
as it inspired the Greek Isiac cult and the Alexandrine
Jews.   Already in the middle of the third century
Hippolytus and Origen speak of Christian "ascetics,"
and we know from Tertullian that virginity and absten-
tion from wine and meat were considered meritorious.
On the other hand self-denial of this kind was probably
practised while living in the world and maintaining the
ordinary relations of life with one's fellow men.   Both
Clement of Alexandria and Tertullian inveigh against
the more eccentric and stricter kinds of asceticism
which were already beginning to be practised apparently
both by Christians and pagans alike[1]; but it was to be
left to the native Egyptian to carry out this method of
life in its extremest degree, and to influence the whole
Christian Church by one of the most remarkable move-
ments the world has ever seen.

We have evidence of pagan hermits in Egypt. One
is mentioned in a papyrus as living in the necropolis of
Sakkara in the second century B.C.[2] There is some reason
to suppose that the first Christian, or one of the first, to
lead the *solitary* life was an Egyptian, Paul the Hermit.
He is said to have fled into the deserts from the Decian
persecution, and to have lived in a cave midway between

---

[1] See Tertullian, *Apolog.* 42.   Clement Alex. *Stromateis*, III. 7.

[2] [Bouché-Leclercq, *Les réclus du Serapéum de Memphis*, in the
Mélanges Perrot; cf. also Weingarten, *Ursprung des Mönchthums im
nachconstantinischen Zeitalter*, Gotha, 1877; Preuschen, *Mönchtum
u. Serapiskult*, p. 5.]

the Nile and the Red Sea; in this cave he died somewhere about the year 340. His biography, attributed to
St Jerome, certainly contains a large element of the
miraculous, but there is no reason to doubt that the
main outlines of the story are quite historical[1]. A
short time before his death he was visited by Antony,
who appears to have held him in the greatest veneration.
The monastery of Deir Mâr Boulos was afterwards
built on the site of his cave; it was visited about the
year 400 by one Postumian, who performed the rôle of
Pausanias in hunting up the early monasteries of
Egypt[2], and, as Dom Butler rightly says, if "the existence
of a monastery of Antony in 375, as vouched for by
Rufinus, is satisfactory evidence of the existence of
St Antony, is it hard to see why the existence of a
monastery of Paul in 400 should not be evidence of the
existence of St Paul the Hermit[3]." Dom Butler,
however, thinks that Paul must have been a unique
example of a hermit living in complete isolation at so
early a date; it is quite true that it is stated in the
Life of Antony that when Antony first became an ascetic
about the year 270, men leading the eremitical life had
not yet gone into the desert but lived in huts in the
neighbourhood of towns, and this points to the fact
that the solitary life was then unknown. On the other
hand it must be remembered that the Decian persecutions in 250 drove hundreds forth from the towns into
the deserts. Of the hunted and solitary lives of these
fugitives we have had a glimpse in the papyri from the

---

[1] See Butler, *Lausiac History*, I. p. 231. Zöckler, *Askese u.
Mönchtum*, 183.

[2] *Sulpicius Severus*, VII.   [3] *Lausiac Hist.* I. p. 232.

Oasis of Kharga, and it is quite possible that deported
suspects and wretches condemned to work in the mines
would find escape to some cavern in the desert hills,
where they might worship their Lord in peace, a happy
release from the afflictions of their persecutors. We
have as yet no direct evidence of this, but it is possible
that we may trace the origin of the solitary movement
back to this period, and it is not improbable that Paul
himself was inspired as a young man by what he had
seen of those living thus far from the haunts of men
and the temptations of the world.

But the man who may be said to have made the
solitary life the ideal of his own and succeeding generations was Antony. His life and exploits have come
down to us in a biography attributed to Athanasius, as
to the genuineness of which there has been some
disagreement in the past. The controversy on this
subject has been prolonged. The traditional view
was that Antony was born about 250, that as a
young man he began to lead an ascetic life, and that he
died at an extreme old age in or about the year 356.
This view was attacked by Weingarten[1] who, as a
corollary to his theory that all the stories about the
ascetics and solitaries of Egypt were monkish fables of
a later date and that no such thing as a monk existed
before the year 340, declared that the Life of Antony was
a pious fraud written by some monk for the purpose of
propagating monastic ideas. He admitted that a person
named Antony certainly had existed, but held that
nobody knew anything about him, and that the other
early ascetics were myths introduced to make a kind of

[1] *Ursprung des Mönchthums*, p. 10 ff.

romance of asceticism. This view had a considerable
following, probably the most important adherent in this
country being Professor Gwatkin[1]. Weingarten's main
argument in support of his thesis was the silence of
Eusebius concerning monks or anything monastic,
and also the fact that the festal letter of Athanasius
written in the year 338 mentions, when referring to
the desert, only Elijah and says nothing of hermits
or solitary ascetics. But Nestle[2] and Zöckler[3] have
pointed out the possibility that the Commentary on the
Psalms attributed to Eusebius contains several references
to monks; and Dom Butler thinks that, apart from the
danger of arguing from the silence of any one writer,
this alone is an important point in the evidence against
Weingarten[4]. It is however from external information,
that is to say from Syrian and Coptic hagiography, and
from the internal criticism of the documents themselves[5],
that the thesis of Weingarten receives the most serious
damage, but it will be better to discuss these points
later when we come to consider in general the sources
of our knowledge of Egyptian monasticism. At present
it is sufficient to say that Weingarten's case against the
genuineness of the Life of Antony stands or falls with
his whole thesis, and this thesis has now been shown to
be untenable. About the question of the authorship
of the "Life of Antony" there is a good deal more
doubt: there seems to be no very good evidence for the

[1] *Studies in Arianism*, pp. 102 and 103.
[2] *Zeitschrift für Kirchengeschichte*, 1882, pp. 504 ff.
[3] *Askese u. Mönchtum*, p. 181.
[4] *Lausiac History*, I. p. 217.
[5] *ib.* p. 220 ff.

authorship of Athanasius himself, although it is possible he may have had a hand in it[1].

Antony, then, was born about the year 250, of Christian parents who were people, apparently, of some small substance; at least they owned some land and possessed slaves. Sozomen tells us that his birthplace was the village of Coma[2] in upper Egypt, but this place has not been identified and the name may perhaps be a mistake that arose from a misunderstanding of the word κώμη. He seems to have been illiterate, nor did he know any Greek. At the age of twenty he was left an orphan, and about this time he first began to be obsessed with ideas of renunciation of the world inspired by hearing the scriptures read in church[3]. "Sell all that thou hast and give to the poor" were words which Antony took as a direct message to himself. Acting on the literal interpretation of the command, he disposed of the property which he had inherited from his parents and, after making due provision for his only sister, handed the proceeds to the needy and outcast. He then took up his abode with a number of men who were practising the ascetic life in huts near the village. It would seem from this that, if there were any *solitary* ascetics as yet besides Paul, Antony had not been brought into contact with them and asceticism was still practised while living in or near the community.

[1] See Zöckler, *Askese u. Mönchtum*, pp. 188 ff.

[2] *Ecclesiastical Hist.* 1. 13.

[3] If Antony were really totally unacquainted with Greek, this implies that there must have been a version of the New Testament in the Egyptian language as early as this date. See art. *Coptic Versions* in Hastings' *Dictionary of the Bible*. [But see also the discussion in *Encyclopaedia Biblica*, col. 5007.]

While here he underwent terrible struggles with the Evil One. It seemed to him that Satan appeared again and again before him under different forms to tempt him: he seems to have thought that he was the prey of the mockery of innumerable devils. He was tortured by doubts as to the wisdom of selling his property and also of leaving his sister, for whom he had a natural and strong affection, nor is it surprising that solitude and self-introspection brought thoughts of lust and the desire for women to a nature begotten of the ardent climate of Egypt.

His method of raising himself superior to these assaults of Satan was characteristically oriental. Unlike the man of Hellenic birth or education who tempered asceticism with personal refinement and the pursuit of knowledge, Antony scorned all such methods in his struggle to keep the soul pure and to crush out the desires of the flesh. To him bodily misery and deprivation was the only method by which these attacks of Satan could be overcome. He continually fasted, often for as much as a week at a time, and deprived himself of sleep, resting when absolutely necessary on the bare ground. He neither washed nor anointed himself, deeming these practices luxurious and unworthy of the true ascetic. By such austerities as these he soon began to attract attention to himself, and this led him to try and make his escape from the world more effectual. He accordingly withdrew to a tomb in the desert hills, not improbably one of the tombs hewn out of the rock in pharaonic times for some long-dead prince or noble, perhaps a worshipper of Osiris and Anubis, gods whom Antony considered devils and evil spirits. Here again he was haunted by the most terrifying voices and visions. He was visited by hordes of devils who smote him with blows and left him in the morning bruised and exhausted. Phantom animals and wild beasts stalked around him in the solitude of his tomb, and devils sought to lure him by chanting the psalms and scriptures in his ear[1]. The extraordinary thing is that with a frame weakened by his ascetic practices he endured this life for twenty years, during which time he maintained a certain native alertness of mind and a shrewd kindness and commonsense which were always at the disposal of young ascetics who came to seek his advice and to try and emulate his ideals. During the persecution of Maximinus in 311 he came boldly forward to minister to Christians cast into prison or condemned to work in the mines. In the meantime his fame had been spread abroad far and wide and he had obtained a great reputation as a worker of miracles. During the Arian controversy which raged during the later years of his life he is said to have been persuaded to leave his desert solitude and to go to Alexandria, where he stoutly preached on behalf of the Athanasian doctrine. Before this he had withdrawn himself into the inner desert and lived in a cave not far from that occupied by his friend and precursor Paul, and here were collected around him a number of disciples, all leading lives of the strictest solitude. This community later became the "monastery of Antony" (Deir Mar Antonios),

---

[1] If, as is probable, the tomb occupied by Antony was one made in pharaonic times it is by no means impossible that the figures of animal headed gods, and scenes in the underworld painted on the walls, became real devils and demons to a mind weakened by fasting.

which exists to this day as does the neighbouring monastery of Paul (Deir Mar Boulos). In spite of a life spent in deprivation and bodily want he lived to an extreme old age to see ascetic communities filled with ardent disciples spring up all over Egypt. He is supposed to have died about the year 356. He had always evinced the greatest hostility towards the Christian custom of mummification and keeping the bodies of the dead embalmed for the inspection of relatives and friends, possibly because this was a contemporary pagan custom and admitted pagan or gnostic irregularities in connexion with the funeral rites. He gave instructions that his body was to be buried in the ground without any preventatives against decomposition.

The influence of Antony on the Christian church of Egypt was enormous. Not long after he had begun the solitary life disciples began to come to him to learn his methods, and they in turn collected disciples of their own until the whole country became scattered with them. The older ideas of asceticism gave way entirely to this new movement. It was no longer considered the highest form of self-abnegation to lead a life vowed to celibacy and to practise austerities with a few other enthusiasts in huts in the neighbourhood of villages or towns. It now became of paramount importance to those who desired to save their souls from the pollution of the world to go forth to the scorching deserts, there to lead a life of prayer and to undergo the greatest possible severities that could be self-inflicted—in short to become a "monk," a μοναχός, one who dwelt alone and wrestled with temptation, weakened by hunger and fatigue, in the awful loneliness of the desert. Nor was

the movement confined to men only.   Antony's sister
is said to have founded a community of women ascetics,
and large numbers of women embraced the solitary life.

Perhaps the two most important communities of
ascetics where enthusiasts retired to live a life like that
of Antony were those situated in the valleys of Nitria
and Skete (Shiēt), desert *wadis* lying south-west of
Alexandria.   That of Nitria was founded by one Am-
monius or Amoun, a contemporary if not an actual
disciple of Antony.   Amoun was the son of rich
parents living in Alexandria.   On the day of his
marriage he and his wife took vows of celibacy and they
lived together for eighteen years as brother and sister.
About the year 320 he withdrew to the desert valley of
Nitria and there remained, only returning to visit his
wife twice a year.   He was soon followed by an ever
increasing number of Christians, who came and lived
each in his own cave or hut and practised, or rather
in their zeal tried to outdo, the austerities of their
neighbours.   This community must have offered a
striking contrast to the luxury and extravagance of the
neighbouring city of Alexandria, but it may be a matter
of some doubt whether their life of squalid misery made
any great appeal to the Greek inhabitants of the city.
If we may judge by names, those of purely native
origin seem to have been the most prominent in Nitria.
The names of Pambo, Harsiesi, Hor, Petubast, Serapion
etc. are all purely Egyptian, and so is that of Amoun,
the founder of the community.   Antony himself,
although bearing a foreign name, seems to have been
of purely Egyptian origin.   The movement was a native
one.

What Amoun did for Nitria, Macarius the Egyptian
(so called to distinguish him from other ascetics of the
same name and of Greek or quasi-Greek origin) did
for the neighbourhood of Skete, and a large community
of the same kind was gathered there soon after the year
330. Each of these communities was called a *laura*.
It is however incorrect to suppose that the *laura* was
in any sense a monastic institution with rules and
regulations which bound the whole community. Each
ascetic was a law unto himself. Those who had recently
joined the community, or the weaker brethren who were
unable to undertake the full severities demanded by the
solitary life, lived in the *laura*, sometimes two together
in a hut, occupying themselves with godly exercises,
repeating the psalms and scriptures and often supporting
life by making mats and weaving flax. At a later date
when Palladius visited Nitria about the year 390, there
were physicians, bakers, a refectory, and a guest house,
but it is probable that these organizations were of later
growth and perhaps influenced by the Pachomian system
which will be referred to later. Some of the monks
however dwelt in caves or "cells[1]" in the inner desert, and
these were hermits indeed, holding no communication
with one another and living in the strictest solitude.
They assembled with the others of the community only
on Saturdays and Sundays for prayer in the church[2].
But of corporate action and a general rule of life for all
there was none. The elder ascetics exercised a general

[1] The "cells" were also sometimes huts, built of rough stones
(Butler, *Lausiac History*, II. p. 25).
[2] See Butler, *Lausiac History*, II. p. 24 ff. *Historia Monachorum*
in Appendix to Vol. I. of same.

authority and gave advice and instructions, but there was
no way of restraining the extravagances of individuals.

As time went on this independence of the individual
was gradually lost owing to the complete or partial
adoption of the Pachomian or cenobitic system, but
mutual independence was certainly the general rule in
the early days of the communities which assembled
round Antony and in the valleys of Nitria and Skete.
Dom Butler has well summed up the spirit of Egyptian
monachism in the following words[1]. "It was a spirit of
strongly-marked individualism. Each worked for his
personal advance in virtue; each strove to do his utmost
in all kinds of ascetical exercises and austerities,—in
prolonging his fasts, his prayers, his silence. The
favourite name used to describe any of the prominent
monks was 'great athlete.' And they were athletes,
and filled with the spirit of the modern athlete. They
loved to 'make a record' in austerities, and to contend
with one another in mortifications; and they would
freely boast of their spiritual achievements. The author
of the *Historia Monachorum* describes the Nitrian monks
as 'surpassing one another in virtues, and being filled
with a spirit of rivalry in asceticism, showing forth all
virtue, and striving to outdo one another in manner of
life.' But it is in Palladius' account of Macarius of
Alexandria that this spirit stands out most conspicu-
ously: 'if he ever heard of any one having performed
a work of asceticism, he was all on fire to do the
same'......Did Macarius hear that another monk ate
nothing but one pound of bread a day? For three
years he ate each day only what he could extract in a

[1] *Lausiac Hist.* I. p. 237.

single handful through the narrow neck of a jar. Did
he hear that the Tabennesiotes ate nothing cooked by
fire throughout Lent? He did the same for seven
years. Did he hear that their general observance was
'great'? He did not rest satisfied until he had gone to
see, and had beaten them all."

While this *solitary* or eremitical movement was fast
growing, monasticism received a new impulse by the
regularization of its ideals due to the genius of Pakhôm.
Pakhôm was born, probably in the year 285[1], of pagan
parents who lived near Esneh in the southern Thebaid.
As a young man of about 20 years old he was enrolled as
a soldier under the emperor Constantine, and on release
from his military service he returned to the Thebaid
and settled down at a village called Khênoboskion,
the native name of which was Shenesēt ("Goosepens")[2].
This was about the year 306. Here, according to some
recensions of his life, he received a divine message in a
vision and was afterwards baptized a Christian. Not
long after he was seized with the desire to lead the
ascetic life, and meeting an aged anchorite named
Palamon, he joined him and began to learn to lead the
life of fasting and prayer. But the Coptic and Arabic
versions add an important detail which the other
versions omit. According to these, when the young
Pakhôm arrived at Shenesēt he found there a small
temple of Serapis, and it was in this that he stayed,
as yet apparently an unconverted heathen, although
moved to take up his abode there by the voice of God.

---

[1] For a discussion of the chronology of Pakhôm's life, see Grützmacher, *Pachomius und das älteste Klosterleben*, pp. 23–33.

[2] By the modern Ḳaṣr eṣ-Ṣayyâd, near Nagʿ Hamâdi.]

He occupied himself while dwelling in the temple with cultivating a small patch of ground, and with growing vegetables for his own needs and those of his poorer neighbours. It was not until after this episode that he was converted and baptized in the neighbouring church. For some time after this he remained with Palamon and the band of ascetics who lived with him, emulating them all in the severity of the discipline and mortifications which he inflicted on himself, and it was not until after eighteen years[1] of the solitary life that he began the foundations of his monastery at Tabennesi, which was to be the first regular monastic institution of Christendom.

Tabennesi lay east of Khenoboskion (the river here runs east and west), and near Denderah; it is not to be confused with the island of Tabenna at Syene[2]. Here under Pakhôm's rule there quickly sprang up an organized community of monks that differed strikingly from the irregular colonies grouped together under the Antonian system. Pakhôm instituted a regular Rule of Life. The monks were all to be employed at some kind of work or trade, and for this purpose they were divided into separate houses. Palladius, who visited the monastery founded by Pakhôm at Akhmim shortly after that at Tabennesi, describes the trades followed as husbandry, gardening, working in bronze, baking, carpentry, fullers' work, dyeing,

---

[1] See Grützmacher, *loc. cit.* p. 29. Dom Butler, *Lausiac Hist.* i. p. 235, places the foundation of Pakhôm's monastery in 305, but he is surely in error here. [The true date must be about 324.]

[2] This mistake was originally due to Sozomen, who wrote Ταβέννη νῆσος for Ταβεννήσιος. Tabennesi was not an island at all.

tanning, calligraphy, and weaving baskets of all sizes. They also learnt the scriptures by heart. Each man was allowed to eat according to his necessities, and might fast also as much as he desired. Work and food were apportioned according to physical abilities. The monks were to sleep three in a cell. There was a common refectory where all might eat together supervised by regular officers. The habit was a cloak girt with a girdle, and a hood or cowl which was to be drawn over the head at meal times in order that each man might be invisible to his neighbour, and silence was the rule at meals. Some monks only ate every second day, some only every third day, and some only every fifth day, but the fasting was entirely optional. Pakhôm said: "Forbid them neither to fast nor to eat." The monks were divided up into grades, each bearing a letter of the alphabet. The scriptures were apportioned off, and so much was to be recited each day. There was a guest house and accommodation for strangers, but monks from outside who desired to enter the brotherhood had to serve a novitiate of three years before entering it[1]. It was, in short, a highly systematized organization and possessed "all the machinery of centralized government, such as does not appear again in the monastic world until the Cistercian and the Mendicant orders arose in the twelfth and thirteenth centuries[2]."

This cenobitic system spread with marvellous rapidity, and attracted not only new members but many of the solitary and unorganized monks who were then imitating

[1] See *Lausiac Hist.* II. p. 87 ff. *Vie de Pakhôme, Annales du Musée Guimet,* XVII. ed. Amélineau.

[2] Dom Butler, *Lausiac Hist.* I. p. 235.

Antony. Monasteries sprang up under the direction of Pakhôm at Peḥbôou, Akhmim, Ṭhebiou and Phenoum, while his sister Maria founded a nunnery for women near Tabennesi and Theodore his pupil a similar institution in connexion with the monastery of Peḥbôou[1]. When Pakhôm died in 345 there were at least eight if not nine monasteries of his foundation, each containing several hundred monks. His system received the approbation of Athanasius, to whom he sent a deputation of monks, and apparently that of Antony too[2]. It is a matter, however, of some doubt whether the apparition of powerful and united communities such as were the Pachomian monasteries was eyed with any favour by the local bishops and clergy. The successors of Pakhôm wielded, as abbots of their monasteries, increasing power, until this culminated in the persons of Shnouti and Bgoul, who in the fifth century stand out as the most powerful ecclesiastical figures of their time outside Alexandria, and who laid the foundations of the national monophysite church as opposed to the orthodox " Melkite " system. Grützmacher[3] has certainly succeeded in showing from the Life of Pakhôm that Pakhôm's relations with the bishops and clergy were not always very amicable, and it is difficult to see how there could have been any other result[4]. In the light of later events the monks appear as hordes of turbulent fanatics who

[1] See Ladeuze, *Étude sur le cénobitisme Pakhomien*, pp. 172–177.

[2] See Grützmacher, *Pachomius und das älteste Klosterleben*, p. 50. Pakhôm and Antony seem never to have actually met.

[3] *Loc. cit.* p. 52 ff.

[4] This is strenuously denied by Père Ladeuze (*Étude sur le cénobitisme Pakhomien*, p. 78 ff.), but without any valid reason so far as one can see.

could be summoned from their desert monasteries to riot
and slay in the streets of Alexandria; in this way they
wielded enormous power, and it is hardly to be doubted
that the organized and disciplined followers of Pakhôm,
even in their earliest days, were a source of uneasiness
to the local bishops.

It may thus be seen that within a hundred years of
the Decian persecution Egypt was dotted all over with
monastic institutions, some being of the unorganized
Antonian type, others of the highly organized cenobitic
type instituted by Pakhôm. The former were mostly
in the north, the latter in the south. Both Antony and
Pakhôm lived to see their methods eagerly adopted by
thousands of their countrymen and the position of the
monks assured as a powerful factor in the history of the
Church. Before however we consider the general importance of this movement let us examine the historical
foundation on which our information rests, for this has
until quite recently been the subject of considerable
controversy among scholars.

The two principal sources containing the history of
early asceticism in Egypt are the works known as *The
Paradise of Palladius*, also called the *Lausiac History*,
and the *Historia Monachorum in Aegypto* attributed
to Rufinus. Latin texts of both these works were first
published by Rosweyde[1], a learned Jesuit of Antwerp
at the beginning of the seventeenth century, and the
Greek text of the former was published by Migne[2].
The *Historia Monachorum* purports to describe a visit

---

[1] *Vitae Patrum*, Books I., II. and VIII. The last is the *Lausiac
History*.

[2] *Patrologia Graec.* XXXIV. Syriac text, *ed.* Budge, 1898.

made by a party of seven persons to some of the most
famous ascetics both in Lower Egypt and the Thebaid.
This took place in the winter of 394–5[1]. Although the
writer describes himself as having been one of the party
throughout the journey, he cannot have been Rufinus
himself, for at the date Rufinus was in the neighbourhood of Jerusalem, and he was also a priest, whereas
the party with the exception of one deacon were all
laymen[2]. Yet there is no doubt that Rufinus wrote
the *Historia Monachorum*[3]. Tillemont thought that
the materials were supplied to Rufinus by Petronius,
afterwards bishop of Bologna, who may have been one
of the party, and this has been accepted by Zöckler[4] and
Grützmacher[5] as the only plausible solution of the
problem. Dom Butler on the other hand thinks that
Rufinus was not the author, and suggests that the work
was compiled by a certain archdeacon Timotheus (not
Timotheus bishop of Alexandria), who was at the time
a monk at Rufinus' monastery on the Mount of Olives
and was afterwards in 412, on the death of Theophilus,
put forward as candidate against Cyril for the patri-
archate of Alexandria[6].

Let us now consider the *Lausiac History* or *Paradise
of Palladius*. In the first place who was Palladius?

[1] For the fixing of this date, see Butler, *Lausiac Hist.* i. p. 10,
note.

[2] See Tillemont, *Mémoires*, xii. 657 ff.

[3] Rosweyde, *Vitae Patrum*, Prolegomenon, iv. par. 10.   Preuschen,
Palladius u. Rufinus, pp. 176–180.

[4] *Askese u. Mönchtum*, pp. 213–215.

[5] *Theol. Literaturzeitung*, 1897. 9.

[6] *Lausiac Hist.* i. Appendix i.   See also Lucius, *Die Quellen der
älteren Geschichte des aegyptischen Mönchtums.* (Brieger's *Zeitschrift
für Kirchengeschichte*, 1885, p. 188.)

A native of Galatia, he was born in the year 367, and when about twenty years old he embraced the monastic life, for by that time the example of the Egyptian monks had spread all over Christendom and was attracting the greatest attention. Palladius resolved to visit the home and birth-place of Christian asceticism, to practise there austerities and mortifications, and see for himself some of the great Egyptian anchorites and hear from their lips reminiscences of the founders of the movement, of Paul, of Antony, of Pakhôm, of Macarius and a host of others. In 388 he arrived in Alexandria, having perhaps spent some time in Cappadocia and Palestine on the way, and after consulting several ascetics who lived in that city he took up his abode in the desert of Nitria. A year later he withdrew into the inner desert and lived with the sterner ascetics who spent their lives in solitude and fasting, in a region called the "cells" from the number of anchorites' abodes which were to be found there. He continued here for about nine years, practising the severest form of the ascetic life first under Macarius of Alexandria and then under Evagrius, making the acquaintance at the same time of many of the leading monks and solitaries. In 400 ill-health compelled him to give up the life in the desert, and he returned to Alexandria and thence went to Palestine. A short time later he was consecrated bishop of Helenopolis in Bithynia, probably by John Chrysostom, whose troubles he afterwards shared. He went to Rome in 404 or 405, where he visited several who were leading the ascetic life in the neighbourhood of the imperial city. Later his connexion with John Chrysostom caused him to be banished to Syene and

the Thebaid. During this exile he spent three years
with the monks who lived in the neighbourhood of
Antinoë.

He returned to Palestine and lived for some time
in the monastery on the Mount of Olives, and in
420 he undertook his work on the ascetics of Egypt,
dedicating it to his friend Lausus who was a chamber-
lain to the emperor Theodosius II. It is from this
dedication that his book has received the title of the
Lausiac History, while so beautiful did the desert
communities appear in the eyes of admirers of the
ascetic life that the narrative also gained the name
of the *Paradise of Palladius*[1]. It contains a series
of biographical sketches of all the famous monks and
ascetics with whom he personally had come into contact during the years he spent in Egypt, or of whom he
heard tales from the lips of disciples and of those who
had known them. The great value of the work is that
it contains the personal experiences of one who had
himself lived with the Egyptian monks in what may
be called the "golden age" of asceticism; it is moreover
singularly free from the miraculous tales which are
usually found in later monkish compilations, and
frankly records the dark side of the picture as well
as the bright. Palladius does not hesitate to relate
instances of monks and nuns who fell from grace and
went off to live a disorderly life in Alexandria, or even
to recall the petty jealousies which occasionally arose
among the women ascetics of a community.

Tillemont set a high value on Palladius' testimony
and considered his veracity on the whole to be above

[1] Tillemont, *Mémoires*, xi. 500 ff.

suspicion.   This idea prevailed until comparatively
lately, when a new school of criticism sprang up under
the leadership of Dr Weingarten.   The latter, as we
have already noted, condemned the Life of Antony as
a " Tendenzschrift," a monkish falsification of the fourth
century written for the purpose of propagating the
monastic ideal, and the *Lausiac History* in his opinion
came under the same heading[1].   Both these works and
the *Historia Monachorum* were the merest fairy tales,
and of no historical value beyond showing that the
origin of asceticism was the solitary life led by the
Egyptians.   He argued from the silence of Eusebius
that no monks can have existed before the year 340.
Dr Lucius a little later endorsed this criticism[2].   The
work of Palladius was a patchwork made up from
various authors, and according to him Palladius sub-
stituted himself for the person of each of these as he
used their experiences.   The elements of the *Lausiac
History* were at the best a few historical facts hidden
in a dense mass of monkish fiction, and it was to be
doubted whether Palladius himself was ever in Egypt
at all.   The criticisms of these two writers threw
considerable doubt on the historical value of our records
of early asceticism and in spite of the protest of Zöckler[3]
they held the field for some time.

Since, however, Weingarten and Lucius wrote, the
texts of both Palladius and Rufinus have undergone

[1] See above, p. 201 f.

[2] *Die Quellen der älteren Geschichte des ägyptischen Mönchtums.*
(Brieger's *Zeitschrift für Kirchengeschichte*, 1885, pp. 192–196.)

[3] Herzog-Plitt, article *Palladius*, see also *Askese und Mönchtum*,
and Article *Asceticism* in Hastings' *Encyclopaedia of Religion and
Ethics.*

thorough investigation at the hands of Dom Butler[1] and
Dr Preuschen[2], while the Life of Pakhôm has in its turn
received new light from the translations from the Coptic
and Arabic of M. Amélineau and from the investigations
of Dr Grützmacher[3] and Père Ladeuze[4]. [We may
therefore regard the scepticism of Weingarten and
Lucius as now exploded, and our knowledge of the
early history of Egyptian monasticism as based on
trustworthy contemporary authorities.

In any case it is evident that to Egypt, with its
deserts to which those weary of the world and anxious
to mortify the flesh could retire, and its rock-cut tombs
which could conveniently serve them as hermits' cells,
the Christian world owes monasticism.]

[1] See above, p. 200, n. 1.
[2] *Palladius u. Rufinus* (Giessen, 1897).
[3] See above, p. 210, n. 1.   [4] See above, p. 213, n. 1.

INDEX

platonized 11; Serapis 34; Unnefer 44; Socharis 102, 104

Painting, the link between Christian and pagan art 143 f.
Pakhôm 210 ff.; his community of monks and the Rule of Life 208 f., 211 ff.
Palamon 210 f.
Palladius 208, 215, 218
Pambo 207
Pamin 123 n.
Panopolites 122
Papnouthios 96
Papyri, magical 42 ff.
Paradise of Adam 164
Paradise of Palladius 214 ff., 217 f.
Paraplex 172
Paul, St 151
Paul the Hermit 199 ff., 203, 205 f.
Peter, apocryphal gospel of 71
Petermann 153
Peter, St 67, 162, 167
Petronius, bp of Bologna 215
Petubast 207
Philip 159
Philo 39 ff.
Pilate 71
Pistis Sophia 111, 127 n., 149 ff., 152 ff., 180 ff., 185, 190, 196 f.
Plato 21, 39
Platonists, later 28 ff.
Plotinus 195
Plutarch 7, 11, 19, 28 f., 31, 33, 51, 59
Pluto 19, 21
Politike 90, 92
Porphyry 194 f.
Postumian 200
Prayers, early 82 f.
Presbyter 7, 90, 93
Preuschen 219
Procession, religious 34 ff.
Prophets 74, 76 ff., 80
Psenosiris 90 ff., 97
Psentheus 102
Ptah-Sokari-Asar 11, 15 f.
Ptolemies, the 2 ff., 26
Ptolemy I (Soter) 17 ff.

Questions of Mary and the Disciples 154
Quietus 104

Ra 12 f., 14, 35 n.
"Ram of Bubastis" 172
Rameses the Great 46
Religion of the Egyptians 2 ff., 7 ff., 42; decay of popular, in Egypt 7; dominated by Osiris 10 f.; least spiritual in world 101
Renan, E. 176
Resurrection 101, 112 f., 125, 131
Rochar 168
Rose, mystic, of Jericho 112
Rosetta Stone 4
Rosweyde 214
Rufinus 200, 214 f.

Sabaoth Adamas 188
Sabarbaphia 196
Sabarbathioneth 196
Sabarbathiot 196
Sabarbathiouth 196
Sabellians 60
Sacrament of the Ineffable One 111
Sacrificati 89
Saints, remains of 105
Salome 66 f., 70
Sandrakottos 18
Sarapion 110, 113 f., 116
Satripis 104
Sayings of Jesus 57 ff., 60 ff., 79
Schmidt, Carl 103, 136, 153 f., 175 f., 183 ff., 193 ff.
Schmiedel 75
Schwartze 153, 176, 183
Sebek 15
Second Peter 77
Seker 182
Septimius Severus 53, 79, 85
Septuagint 38, 96
Serapeum at Sakkara 20
Serapion 207; of Antioch 71
Serapis 2, 22, 24, 28 f., 32, 42, 51, 92, 210; cult of 18 ff.
Set 8 ff., 12, 29, 43 f., 137, 140
Seth 193 ff.

For EU product safety concerns, contact us at Calle de José Abascal, 56–1°, 28003 Madrid, Spain or eugpsr@cambridge.org.

www.ingramcontent.com/pod-product-compliance
Ingram Content Group UK Ltd.
Pitfield, Milton Keynes, MK11 3LW, UK
UKHW012331130625
459647UK00009B/206